D0965710

A Butler's Guide to
Entertaining

A Butler's Guide to
Entertaining

Nicholas Clayton

BATSFORD

This edition published in 2016 by
Batsford, an imprint of Pavilion Books Company Ltd
1 Gower Street
London WC1E 6HD

First published in 2011 by National Trust Books

ISBN: 9781849943758

A CIP catalogue record for this book is available from the
British Library.

20 19 18 17 16
10 9 8 7 6 5 4 3 2 1

Printed by Toppan Leefung Printing Ltd, China

This book can be ordered direct from the publisher at the website:
www.pavilionbooks.com, or try your local bookshop.

For JD

CONTENTS

INTRODUCTION

Entertaining means different things to different people but there is no doubt that the downturn in the economy and the rise over the last decade or so of the celebrity chef has rekindled an interest in all things culinary and encouraged the great British public back indoors to start cooking and entertaining. Entertaining is not all about eating and drinking but whatever form of entertainment we choose – they are always inextricably linked. Cinemas can earn as much from popcorn sales in the foyer as they do from the tickets. However, eating out as a form of entertainment has become a very expensive option for many people, which is another good reason to stay in.

Eating and drinking are vital, that much is understood, and they provide us with the energy to carry on doing what it is we are really here for. Entertaining is a pleasurable thing to do, or at least it should be, and provides us with an opportunity to group together and socialise. Virtually every gathering, from the christening and wedding reception to the wake, in some way centres around, or ends up with, us showing one another some form of hospitality.

Entertaining guests, friends and family is a perfect opportunity to show kindness and generosity; it is an extension of ourselves and, in a business setting, the level and quality of the hospitality provided can often make or break a deal. For years entertaining has been a chance for some people to flaunt wealth and power with professionally organised parties getting bigger and bigger, and set in more and more exotic locations with costs running into thousands of pounds. To show kindness and generosity you don't really need a lot; bigger and more expensive doesn't necessarily mean better. Some of the best parties I've ever been to have been in back gardens or top-floor flats.

Entertaining is all about how well you treat your guests and how welcome you make them feel. It all starts with the planning.

Nicholas Clayton

PREPARING
FOR THE PARTY

OUTSIDE ASSISTANCE?

Planning a simple party at home shouldn't create any
great problems but some people will opt for outside
assistance because they may not want the stress of
entertaining on a larger scale. You may be looking
for a suitable venue, perhaps a marquee in your
own garden, and outside catering.

Choosing venues and caterers

If you are planning a wedding it can be reasonably
straightforward and there are numerous organisers
to choose from. A corporate event may pose a few
problems of its own, but the planning is very similar.

First, determine your objectives, a location and a date,
then make a list of people you want to invite, and plan
to send the invitations as early as possible to be sure
the most important guests can attend.

The next thing to do is to find an appropriate venue.
As the outside caterer and the venue are the two most
important elements, it is a good idea to organise both
at the same time.

The list of possible venues is endless with conference
centres, hotels, marquees and reception halls to choose
between, but whatever you decide to do, remember that
too much space is as bad as not enough.

Choosing an outside caterer can be a difficult decision. Get at least two or three estimates, or choose by recommendation. Go and see them at an event if you can before deciding. Have a look at the equipment they use and the general attitude of the staff and the caterer.

If the venue you choose provides catering, so much the better, but if they are separate it is very important that you get the two to liaise. Sit down with the caterer and the venue company and discuss in fine detail exactly what you want, and who will do what. Try to have as flexible a budget as possible because very often final costs can be double your initial estimates!

Most companies, photographers, entertainers and guest speakers will accept bookings up to a year in advance so it's best to book as early as possible, especially if your event falls in or around any of the peak times.

If you employ an outside company for any event, remember that it is often expected that you provide food and drinks for the staff. And don't forget to offer the band or entertainment refreshment of some sort during the proceedings as well.

Hiring bylaws and council requirements can be complex so find out as much as possible before you sign anything and read the small print carefully. For example, if you hired a venue until midnight and you are not able move everything out by that time, you could be charged extra or even fined as it could be that another event company has to set up straight after you.

Choosing a marquee

*Marquee (Ma:'ki) n. A large tent. From French
marquise and mistaken in English as a plural. Linen
canopy placed over an officer's tent to distinguish it
from others, originally marchioness.*

There is definitely something atmospheric about a
marquee; maybe it's the unmistakeable smell when you
first walk into one, especially one set up on grass in high
summer. Of course, a beer tent has a very special smell
all of its own.

Marquees were traditionally used for outdoor events such
as weddings, garden parties and country fêtes,
but there are many other times when a large tent
would be useful for a party because as well as looking
terrific in a country setting it can be a very cost-effective
way of extending the house to accommodate large groups
of people.

There are many types of marquees and they differ in
shape and size depending on the structure and holding
capacity. Better quality marquees are made from a type
of PVC for durability and most are based around three
basic styles: traditional central pole; side poles and guide
ropes; or with an aluminium frame without poles, which
is easier to erect almost irrespective of terrain. Another
variety is the high-peak frame tent, generally with a steel
frame and no poles, which has fewer parts and a much
higher top. All types of marquees are available in a variety
of colours although the majority are white. The size and

shape you choose not only depends on the space you have available but also on the amount of people you want or need to accommodate. You can have them floored out with a solid dance floor, to avoid getting stilettos stuck in the lawn, and set up with rows of seats for a presentation or with tables and chairs for dinner.

Hiring a butler

I'm probably biased and why not, but hiring a traditional butler for a party has never been known *not* to impress the guests. The experienced hand of the trained butler is hard to beat when you need professional help. It may not cost as much as you might think, and for the added luxury of knowing your guests will be expertly looked after, hiring in a butler is worth every penny.

Be very clear exactly what it is you want the butler to do before hiring. Check out as many agencies and websites as possible to find a suitable person; butlers can be male and female these days. A properly trained butler can be relied upon to deliver an outstanding service and, if asked, will probably drive people home as well. A perfectly dressed butler handing around glasses of Champagne is something your guests are not likely to forget.

Deliverance
A couple of years ago I was asked to butler at a private clay pigeon shoot in the West Country. The party was to mark the Glorious Twelfth, the day in August that marks the start of the season when grouse becomes fair game

and can be hunted legally until December. I was to do lunch, afternoon tea and a semi-formal dinner in the evening and, as I was assured nothing living was actually going to be shot, I agreed.

The first shoot-out over, lunch was served with salads, cold meats and cold poached salmon, bread straight from the oven, with homemade lemonade for those on guns and Pimm's for the others.

After lunch a few people left and I heard someone say 'We're one short in our team; ask the butler to join in'. I went to the door and protested with 'I've the tea to do', but before I could come up with a really good excuse I was handed a shotgun and told where to stand. 'Pull!' someone shouted and up went the first clay and I missed; the next one I quickly had in my sights and hit it fair and square. My accuracy held and I demolished the next four.

Slightly hearing impaired and with ringing in my ears, I served afternoon tea. Scones, clotted cream and strawberry jam, Victoria sponge, coffee and walnut cake and pots of Darjeeling. Then, with the refreshing and restorative effects of the tea having taken effect, during the next round I hit every clay bar one.

Dinner started with Champagne and prize-giving, followed, almost predictably, by a smoked grouse salad. I was placed just behind the winner, only one point off the title, and received some very suspicious looks from the professionals when my name was read out.

Apart from the smoked grouse, which had been sent from a store in London, everything I had served during the day and in the evening had been ordered online and delivered on time by a well-known supermarket and was ready to use, pre-washed and in part pre-cooked, all of the highest quality, with only minimal preparation required. It's not cheating, it's a brilliant idea and precisely why a party service is designed. It's high street outside catering really, and although it obviously comes at a price, it's worth it, all perfectly fresh and extremely well presented. It makes clearing up very easy and gave me the opportunity to join in the entertainment without compromising anything.

INVITATIONS

Once you have sorted out your venue and catering arrangements, it's time to send out the invitations.

His Nibs

Making an impact by handwriting your invitations is very personal and using a fountain pen is very smart. The pen is the original mobile communication tool, said to be mightier than the sword and certainly a lot more chic than an email.

There are obviously dozens of ways of producing invitations and, provided you are not restricted by anything, you can say whatever you like. Just ensure that you add the important bits even for a simple garden party, such as a dress code if there is one, and the time and the place.

John and Jane
....

You are invited to James and Clare's annual end-of-summer barbecue in the garden at our house

Saturday 30th August from about 3.30pm

RSVP James or Clare on usual numbers

You can also send handwritten invitations for events such as business or formal dinners but they are often printed with the invited names added by hand. Wedding invitations are nearly always printed and, although there are modern alternatives, they are traditionally worded as follows:

```
Invitation

Mr and Mrs Smith request the pleasure of the
company of

............................ *Mr David Jones* ............................

at the marriage of their daughter Jane
to
Mr John Brown
at
The Church, Clifton, Bristol
on
Saturday 10th May at 2 o'clock
and reception afterwards at The Grand Hotel.


RSVP by 15th March
Address
Email + phone number
```

Send the invitation in good time and, depending on the formality of the occasion, anywhere from two to eight weeks in advance. For wedding invitations in particular some people are now sending 'Save the Day' cards up to a year in advance before the event and then formal invitations about three months in advance. Include a map with the invitation, as they're invaluable for those people unfamiliar with the area and SatNav is not always reliable.

A business or a product launch invitation could look something like this:

Mr David Jones

The Fine Wine Company
requests the pleasure of your company to
celebrate the launch of our new range and
to enjoy some fine wines and champagne.

Date: Tuesday 2nd March
Time: 5–8pm
Venue: The Showroom, Regent Street,
London

Dress code, smart casual

RSVP by February 25th
E-mail
Telephone

Website

A final thought: If you send printed invitations and find
that half of your guests cannot attend, be very wary about
phoning around to make up numbers. If the people you
call get the slightest inkling that they are in some way
afterthoughts they may well feel insulted and then decline.

SET DESIGNING

Once the invitations are out and replies start coming in, you can start to plan how you want your party to look.

Linen

Probably more to do with cost and user-friendliness than anything else, most table linen is not actually linen but is instead made from cotton or a blend of cotton, linen and a hard-wearing material such as polyester. Linen is still the generic term applied to all textiles – tablecloths, napkins, tray cloths and placemats or anything else of a similar nature – used in the dining room.

Tablecloths

Never forget, before you do anything else, to check that the table is stable. You don't want it to collapse as your guests sit down.

Tablecloths must be the right size for the table and to allow for the correct amount of overhang; generally the longer the table the deeper the overhang. A formal table can have an overhang ranging from 30–46cm (12–18in).

If you put a cloth on a table and find that there is even the faintest of marks that could be seen by your guests, remove the cloth and use another one, although you could have a go at a spot clean if there is time. Never attempt to hide a mark under a glass or a plate. A tablecloth should not have creases and, again, if you have time, iron out any folds before you use the cloth. If folds are visible, lay the cloth on the table so that the folds are parallel with the table sides or ends and so that there is one centre fold running the full length of the table. If the folds are not parallel the cloth will look haphazard and scruffy and the overhang will not be correct.

You can use a silence cloth on the table, which is a type of lining cloth that can be placed on to the table before the tablecloth and should overhang the table sides by at least 8cm (3in). Lining cloths are made of a fairly thick felt or a soft, smooth spongy material and you can buy lengths of it in major department stores. They are particularly useful if the table has a surface that needs to be evened up or protected from possible bumps, scratches and scrapes.

If, in the case of a very long table or where you have to join tables together, you have to use more than one tablecloth to cover it all, use the same size and colour cloths and overlap them with about a 15cm (6in) overlap. Make sure that the overhang is absolutely the same all the way round; you should not be able to see where one cloth starts and the other finishes. At a formal dinner party overlap the cloths so that the top edge of the overlap across the table is not visible to the diners as they come into the dining room; that way it will flow and appear like one cloth.

If you use a linen hire company, order your requirements in good time. Check as soon as possible that you have

Guide to tablecloth sizes

		table	cloth
Square	Seats 4	70–102cm (28–40in)	132 x 132cm (52 x 52in)
Round	Seats 4	91–122cm (36–48in)	152 x 152cm (60in) dia
	Seats 6	112–142cm (44–56in)	173–178cm (68–70in) dia
	Seats 6	117–147cm (46–58in)	178–183cm (70–72in) dia
	Seats 6–8	163–193cm (64–76in)	224–229cm (88–90in) dia
Oblong	Seats 4–6	102 x 147cm (40 x 58in)	127 x 178cm (50 x 70in)
	Seats 6–8	122 x 183cm (48 x 72in)	178 x 229cm (70 x 90in)
	Seats 8–10	122 x 229cm (48–90in)	178 x 264cm (70 x 104in)
	Seats 12–14	122 x 274cm (48–108in)	178x 305cm (70 x 120in)
Oval	Seats 4–6	102 x 147cm (40 x 58in)	132 x 178cm (52 x 70in)
	Seats 6–8	122 x 178cm (48 x 70in)	178 x 229cm (70 x 90in)
	Seats 8–10	122 x 229cm (48 x 90in)	178 x 264cm (70 x 104in)
	Seats 12–14	122 x 274cm (48 x 108in)	178 x 305cm (70 x 120in)

received exactly what you ordered, even if this means opening the bags before the delivery person has gone to be absolutely sure. Never leave checking to the last minute; you can seldom get a delivery an hour before dinner.

Count the hired items into the house and count them out again just to put your mind at rest that you haven't sent back any of your own things.

Store your own tablecloths in acid-free tissue paper and not in plastic bags as the plastic tends to cause mould if left for any length of time. Iron the cloths with a scrupulously clean iron and one that is not too hot to avoid scorching the linen.

Napkins

Table napkins should be handled as little as possible before they are placed on the table and should be immaculately laundered and ironed if made from fabric; they are used, after all, to clean around the mouth and should be pristine. There are dozens of fancy ways to fold table napkins and this seems to be regarded as some sort of art form, but a flat, simply folded, well-ironed linen napkin will always outsmart creations like swans, miniature hats and fans sticking out of wine glasses.

At breakfast you can set whatever shape you like but, in common with afternoon tea, a napkin folded to resemble a triangle with the middle point set facing west is probably right. (An afternoon tea napkin is normally half the size of those used for breakfast, lunch and dinner, see page 83.) I seldom use linen for breakfast because cloth never seems to mop jammy fingers quite like paper. Paper is arguably not the most environmentally conscious choice, but it can be recycled and in the long run it saves a washing-machine load.

Table setting for breakfast

This is a simple set up with tools on the table that you think your guests will need and then it's up to you how you serve it. You could serve breakfast as in a bed and breakfast or arrange a small buffet and let your guests fend for themselves. The latter definitely gets my vote, providing you can keep cooked items warm in some sort of warmer or on hotplates. You can always cook things to order if you need to. A cup and saucer with a teaspoon and a glass for juice are essential and fairly obvious, as are a bread plate and a napkin.

Table setting for lunch

Lunch is generally less formal than dinner, at least for most people. There may not be so many courses but the table is set in much the same way as for dinner. There would be more cutlery for lunch than shown in the below illustration, which has been drawn to illustrate how to set a round table. For lunch you could expect, for example, to place a soup spoon or, instead, another smaller knife and fork for a starter and a perhaps a pudding spoon and fork. Most of the time only two glasses are placed at lunch, one for water and one for a wine.

Salt and pepper pots should be placed at intervals around the table whenever the table is laid, one set per three to four people, and place a low seasonal floral decoration in the middle of the table if you think it appropriate.

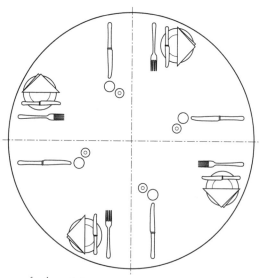

Table setting for dinner

Make sure your cutlery is clean and well polished.
Dried egg yolk stuck in between the tines of forks is
unforgivable, along with fingerprints and smears from a
badly functioning dishwasher. To avoid leaving your dabs
on the silver when you are setting the table, never touch
any part of it that is used to eat; that is to say the blades
of knives, the fork's tines and the bowls of spoons.

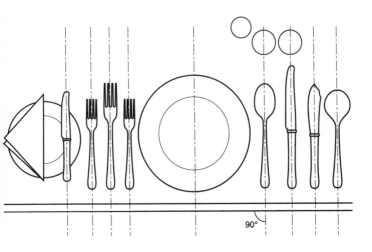

As already noted we eat with our eyes and a well-set
table with shining cutlery is all part of the theatre. Check
that every piece of cutlery and every place setting is
parallel to the next and exactly the same distance from
the edge of the table. If you don't take care when doing
this it can look as if you just threw it all on the table.

Glassware

All of the glassware you put on the table for every setting must be perfectly clean. If you spot a mark don't breathe on the glass as you would to polish your reading glasses. Checking and re-polishing your glasses before your guests arrive is a time-consuming but necessary task.

A great time saver and an old butler trick is to fill a large teapot with boiling water and remove the lid. Hold each glass to be cleaned over the open pot; the steam coats the glass making it really easy to polish with an immaculately clean lint-free teacloth.

There are many ways of placing glasses on a table and the illustration opposite shows one. Generally glasses are set out for ease of access. It's difficult for the diner to access shorter glasses if they are placed behind and further away than the taller ones.

If you imagine an area divided into four equal squares you can place one glass in each square. Place the glass for water just in front of the point of the main-course knife, but not too close; about the width of your index finger is about the right distance. Then place the glass for white wine to the left of it and slightly out in front. In the square above the white-wine glass, place the taller red-wine glass and, out to the left of the square, the remaining space is reserved for other glasses, such as Champagne. When you have finished, have a look from one end of the table and check that every glass is in line; this may seem a little pedantic, but if the line is ragged it just doesn't look good.

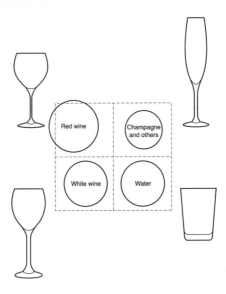

Table-top flower arrangements

Flowers and all things horticultural brought into the house add drama and style, and play an important role in staging a party, but they do not necessarily have to cost the earth or be enormous.

Put cut flowers into lukewarm water; there is less oxygen in it so it reduces the amount of gas bubbles taken up by the stems and thereby maximises their water uptake. The only exceptions to this rule are spring-flowering bulbs such as tulips and hyacinths, which seem to prefer and react well to a vase of cold water.

Cut the stems to the required length and at an angle, to increase water absorption and prevent the stems sealing themselves on the bottom of the vase.

If you are preparing a regular vase, one that is not designed for a table decoration, cut at least 2.5cm (1in) off stems, as this reinvigorates the flowers. If you find a packet of flower food stuck to the wrapping, it's a good idea to use it. It lengthens the bloom's life and goes some way to holding back any premature wilt. Some of the old tricks, like adding carbonated lemonade or an aspirin don't work, although crushing the very ends of rose stems and then plunging them into boiling water for a few moments is said to lift the heads for a while.

Table arrangements should be kept fairly simple. There is a current trend towards bigger and bolder – I'm definitely all in favour of bringing the garden indoors but setting up floral arrangements to rival those of a Chelsea Flower Show medallist could be too much.

It is obviously important to be able to see the person across the table so a good rule is to keep the arrangements not so low that they are insignificant and not so high that the diners can't see one another.

Be careful when wrapping or draping foliage around candles and candelabras, as when the candles burn down things can burst into flames in a flash. It happened to me once at a party in a marquee and I had to use the contents of an ice bucket to douse the flames.

Lighting

Candles placed in candlesticks or in candelabras should always be new; don't be tempted to re-light half-burnt old ones as this doesn't look good and the candles probably won't last for the whole dinner. If the candlesticks are silver give them a quick polish.

New candles should fit well into the candlestick holders. You will not get a successful fit if the holders are full of old wax from previous dripping and a good tight fit is recommended just in case someone jogs the table and the candles jump out of their seats.

Don't scratch old cold wax off candlesticks with a knife. De-wax metal candlesticks by holding the candlestick holders in a sink of hot water with washing-up liquid. This is a very effective way of softening the wax and de-greasing at the same time. Immerse as much of the candlestick as is required to remove old wax but do not sink the whole thing. Some candlesticks have felt or velvet fixed to the bottom; if this is allowed to get wet it takes some time to dry, and if it is placed on a polished wood table it will leave marks.

Check when all the candles are in position that they are upright and parallel to one another. You can expect to need two to four candelabras depending on the length of the table. Make sure that the flames will not be at eye level, which is uncomfortable for the guests.

Candles are lit just before the diners come into the
dining room and are not put out until they leave. You
should always light candles with a lighter to avoid the
smell of matches lingering.

Interior decorating

Decorating the party area is down to personal taste and
type of event but if you are on a budget, nothing is as
effective as balloons, which are cheap, available in all
colours and can be very effective *en masse*.

MAKING YOUR GUESTS FEEL RELAXED

Place cards

Place cards are the roof-shaped folds of stiff paper with
the guest's name on that you will usually see on tables at
a wedding reception or sometimes at business functions.
They are not really needed for a smaller party.

Whatever the event, the way you set out the table may
not suit everyone and if your guests decide to change the
place cards around, don't be insulted, worry too much or
even say anything; they probably have a perfectly good
reason for doing so.

Relaxed seating plans and not getting too stressed about the etiquette of the occasion is the way to go. Many of the rules were established in the courts of kings and queens and were perpetuated for generations by wealthy people, but nowadays for the more liberally minded the do's and don'ts are far less important. However, there is no getting away from the importance of table manners (which are dealt with in the chapter on being a good guest, see page 157).

Guest of honour

The guest of honour is someone you feel deserves the accolade and a special place at the table. It could be the newlyweds of course in the case of a wedding, a foreign visitor or perhaps an elderly parent.

There are guidelines as to their position at the table. A female guest of honour normally sits to the right of the host and a male guest of honour sits to the left of the hostess. The host and hostess in this case would sit at opposite ends of the table.

With only one guest of honour, seat the host and the guest at opposite ends, female guests of honour opposite the hostess, and for a male guest of honour, seat him opposite the host. The remaining host can sit anywhere as there are no hard-and-fast rules regarding their position for an informal, relaxed dinner party.

Seating plan

If the party is a big one, such as a wedding where you have several tables, a seating list set up near the entrance to the dining room is a good idea; it helps the guests find their table faster and it's better than having them line up as if they are at school. Then at the table add a place card to direct the guest to exactly the right seat.

Old fashioned it may be and some men may feel a little self-conscious doing it, but it's still a nice gesture for the men to pull the chairs out and help to seat the ladies, together with helping them on with their coats when leaving.

The top table seating plan at a wedding reception can create problems should the parents be divorced but traditionally the seating positions are as follows:

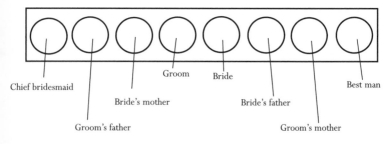

Chief bridesmaid
Groom's father
Bride's mother
Groom
Bride
Bride's father
Groom's mother
Best man

If the bride's parents are divorced and remarried it goes like this:

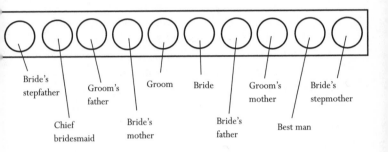

Bride's stepfather | Chief bridesmaid | Groom's father | Bride's mother | Groom | Bride | Bride's father | Groom's mother | Best man | Bride's stepmother

If the groom's parents are divorced and remarried it goes like this:

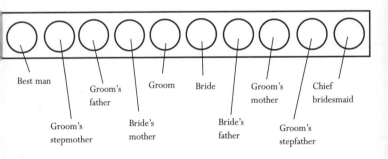

Best man | Groom's stepmother | Groom's father | Bride's mother | Groom | Bride | Bride's father | Groom's mother | Groom's stepfather | Chief bridesmaid

Another, possibly less contentious, option is for the bride and groom to host their own top table with the best man, ushers and bridesmaids and then simply allocate another table near the top for all the parents.

Menu

A menu is not necessary unless the occasion calls for one, such as a wedding. It is not usual to have one at less formal gatherings so if you are not careful it could look a bit silly and if something has to be changed everyone will know. If the party is a formal one a menu can be a good idea to discreetly forewarn the guests as to exactly what is planned, when the speeches will be or perhaps to direct everyone away from the table for the dessert.

Timing

Timing is important even for a dinner party at home but if the occasion is a little more formal and you're the organiser, you need to get things moving. Pour water into the water glasses before your guests sit down, then once they are seated pour some wine and make sure that the gaps between the first two courses are short. Be especially aware if you have a diabetic in the group because it could be that they have to eat fairly quickly. I know only too well from experience that nothing riles diners more than having to wait for a long time between courses. You would be surprised how even the calmest of dinner guests can turn on you, if kept waiting.

A lot of people like the chance to get up for a while before the dessert is served and a few still like to slip out of sight to light up a cigarette. You could decide to serve the dessert as a buffet so that the guests can choose what they want and when they want it for themselves; they then have the opportunity to leave the table.

Table service

Look after the oldest person first and then the ladies; obvious and old fashioned maybe but always best. The lady sitting to the right of the host is served first and then service continues around the table in a clockwise direction, then the host is served. Sometimes the order of service is decided upon by the host or hostess and may not necessarily follow the norm.

If you are hiring the services of a butler, expect your guests to be offered their dinner from various serving plates from their left. The guest simply picks up the serving cutlery and takes as much or as little as they like. Silver service is similar except that the guest won't be offered their dinner; it will be given to them. Plates will disappear like magic from the right when guests have finished and they should expect to be served drinks from the right.

RULES OF
ENGAGEMENT

MEETING AND GREETING

Meeting and greeting your guests is an extremely important element of hospitality. Although in some places it may have gone a bit out of fashion, like manners and common courtesy, it should not be underestimated or ignored.

'Nice to see you, how are you, let me get you a drink' is a very easy opening line. Some parties are so busy and so crowded that it will be almost impossible for the hosts to greet each guest individually. It's worth a try though, because not all your guests will have the confidence to just strut in and mingle – for some the whole thing can be very intimidating, so a greeting from the host can be nicely reassuring.

A kiss or a handshake?

Men generally shake hands when they meet, although some men meeting good friends may adopt the bear hug, the force of which you have to be ready for and adopt a sort of brace position. It's acceptable for women to kiss each other on the cheek if they know each another well enough, although that Hollywood style 'mwaw mwaw' greeting can seem a little shallow and insincere. It's certainly acceptable for a man to kiss a woman in greeting like this but she doesn't necessarily have to accept it and if she doesn't he shouldn't be insulted. It should not be a full-blown lips to the cheek affair anyway, which you can reserve for your nearest and dearest; it's more a gesture really, as you go cheek across cheek.

The amount of times you do the cheek across cheek movement differs depending on where you are; in Britain and in some parts of Europe a kiss once on each cheek is acceptable, but in parts of Italy, Switzerland and elsewhere, a third one seems to be the norm.

For some, this kissing routine can be a nervous moment and actually knowing whether to do it or not can be difficult; a slight bending towards the other person or the other person slightly bending towards you is normally signal enough that it's safe to do it, but once or twice you might find you bend forward slightly to kiss the other person and they have pulled back, which may be some sort of social position signalling and should not be taken personally.

Long acceptable in other places, and in other cultures, it seems that most Englishmen still find a cheek-to-cheek greeting like this from another man a bit odd, and would prefer just to shake hands.

But men should be gentle with their handshakes; don't treat a woman as if you were meeting a truck driver, and be especially careful if the person is elderly.

Should you be faced at any time with a member of the Royal family, don't offer your hand first. You should wait until they offer theirs and then you may shake. In the case of the Queen this shake should last only a second or so and it should be very gentle.

How to shake hands

The style and quality of a man's handshake is very important and sends very clear signals: be firm but gentle with women but shake another man's hands as if you mean it; there is really nothing worse than shaking a limp, clammy, lifeless hand – a handshake should be full of character.

Offer your entire hand and grip palm to palm. Look straight in the other person's eyes when you shake their hand; looking anywhere else is extremely rude and more or less shows your disinterest in that person. Nothing makes this more obvious than glancing across the room just at the moment you shake or spotting someone else with whom you would rather be in conversation.

Coats

It's a good idea to think about where you want to put your visitors' coats in advance because there is nothing worse than a pile on someone's bed or up the stairs. If you have staff for the evening, allocate the job to someone so that they can organise the hanging up on arrival and the handing back on departure and, if needs be set up a decent rail with plenty of hangers. If there is a butler around he or she will normally see to it.

Being a good host

The number-one rule to remember is that you are the host and as such it is your primary duty to ensure the comfort of your guests. Look after everyone, particularly those who may find it difficult to socialize, make sure they are comfortable and that all of your guests have what they need.

DRINKS:
THE LOGISTICS

ESTIMATING DRINKS QUANTITIES

When organising a reception or a large party decide
how many bottles you think you will need and of what
they should comprise. It is best to do this for smaller
gatherings too. If you are having outside caterers you can
discuss this beforehand, as they will have a pretty good
idea of how much to bring, but if you are providing the
catering yourself then you will definitely need to work
out how many alcoholic drinks and how many soft drinks
your guests are likely to want.

It can be surprising how many bottles of wine a fairly
simple dinner party of about fourteen people can
consume, so it is a good idea to keep another couple
of cases at the ready and close to the dining room.

It is also vitally important to have the right amount of
glasses. There's nothing worse than having to rush out
to wash a batch because you have run out. It is easy at a
dinner party because the glasses are already on the table
and, apart from one or two each for the pre-dinner
drink, you know how to quantify.

Big receptions are different and it often happens that
the waiters go around with trays of drinks and the
guests take a glass each time. If they do it three times,
the collection of empty glasses is slightly out of sync and
you have 80 guests, that amounts to about 240 glasses,
not counting the 50 per cent who, over the course of
the reception, take four or even five glasses.

The aperitif or welcome drink

Pre-dinner or welcome drinks are generally kept quite simple with very little choice. If you offer a pre-dinner drink as a sort of *fait accompli* most people will go for what you have suggested. If you offer a glass of Champagne, this is nearly always acceptable, unless a guest is driving or doesn't drink alcohol, so have some soft drinks available as well. A few bottles of beer and a bottle of white wine are worth keeping in the fridge as an alternative.

At parties in Europe, it is often the case that only Champagne, white wine and the occasional beer are served, together with water for those who don't drink alcohol, and this seems perfectly adequate.

For non-drinkers and children you might like to keep chilled, fresh-pressed fruit juice and some bottles of still and sparkling mineral water at hand.

Champagne
This is probably the best reception drink ever. There is nothing quite like a freezing cold glass of Champagne to kick a party off. Poured properly there are approximately six to seven glasses in a bottle. Allow one or two glasses per person, but have a couple of chilled bottles in reserve.

For more on Champagne, and other sparkling wines, see page 53.

Buck's Fizz

Champagne and orange juice is a great drink.
The orange improves the Champagne. The Champagne
definitely improves the orange.

Philip, Duke of Edinburgh

Still seen at some parties and weddings, just mix Buck's
Fizz as you go, about half and half Champagne and orange
juice. This obviously doubles the amount of people you
can serve with one bottle of Champagne but also means
you have to buy some decent orange juice.

Pimm's No. 1 Cup

This is a summer garden-party drink. According to the
instructions on the bottle you should 'mix one part
Pimm's spirit drink with three parts chilled lemonade
and serve with lots of ice'. To add to the flavour add
pieces of orange, mint, cucumber, strawberries, apples
and lemon. With around 2 litres (3½ pints) of clear
carbonated lemonade, a bottle of Pimm's makes about
fourteen servings. Allow approximately two glasses
per person.

Pimm's No. 3 Winter Cup

Not just for summer, Pimm's is great warmed up in the
autumn and winter months. Use apple juice instead of
lemonade, about three parts apple juice to one part
Pimm's Winter. Warm in a pan (without any fruit)
and serve in heat-resistant glasses. Perfect for a bonfire
party and a very pleasant alternative to glühwein.

Drinks during dinner

Wine
You are generally advised to allow three glasses of wine per person when dining but you should probably plan for more; there are approximately six glasses of wine per bottle. Decide on the proportions of red and white wine you will require.

H_2O
Have plenty of jugs of chilled water available for the table. Tap water has a much lower carbon footprint than bottled water, though some prefer bottles of still and carbonated mineral water.

Non-alcoholic alternatives
It is always useful to have a stock of non-alcoholic drinks to hand. Many people don't drink alcohol for all manner of reasons and should never be made to feel as if they should fit in by taking a drink. If someone doesn't want a drink and says no, that's what they mean. There is an enormous selection of soft drinks on the market and, again, if you know who is coming and what they like you can buy accordingly. If you don't drink but you really think you should 'fit in' and look as if you are drinking, there are some very good low- or no-alcohol wine lookalikes available and some non-alcoholic lagers that look the part – some really do taste the same.

Children can consume a phenomenal amount of fizzy drink if allowed, but to avoid the chance of any unexpected cases of 'many happy returns' and the subsequent clearing up I restrict the fizz to water and mix it with a good-quality cordial or fruit juice, which is far better than those carbonated concoctions that look more like hazardous waste.

Lemonade

150g (5½oz) caster sugar
8 unwaxed lemons – about 350ml (12fl oz) juice
  and the zest of 2

Place the sugar and lemon zest into a saucepan and add 125ml (4fl oz) of water. Heat gently and stir until the sugar has dissolved, then boil for 3–4 minutes until syrupy. Cool for 10 minutes then stir in the lemon juice and add 750ml (1¼ pints) of water. Pour into clean, empty bottles and chill until very cold.

Toasts

If you are going to serve Champagne or possibly a sparkling wine for a toast, allow one glass per person. This is about one bottle for every six guests but if you pour carefully and just enough for the toast, you can stretch it a bit further: about half a glass is fine.

OPENING AND SERVING DRINKS

Champagne

I drink Champagne when I'm happy and when I'm
sad. Sometimes I drink it when I'm alone. When I have
company I consider it obligatory. I trifle with it if I'm
not hungry and drink it when I am. Otherwise I never
touch it, unless I'm thirsty.

Madame Lily Bollinger

The pressure inside a bottle of Champagne is said to be
between 85 and 100 pounds per square inch (*c.*620kPa),
which is roughly equivalent to the pressure in the rear
tyre of a red London double-decker bus.

To withstand this pressure, the bottle is made of thicker
and heavier glass than a normal wine bottle and has a
specially designed dimple in the bottom, the punt, to
help take the strain. The pressure is also the reason for
the cork being wired in place, as anyone who has ever
taken the wire off a shaken bottle without holding the
cork down will already know.

Opening Champagne
It may seem boring, but to be absolutely correct you
should never hear a Champagne cork 'pop' when you
open it. It may be acceptable for a Formula One Grand
Prix winner to spray fizzed-up Champagne everywhere,
but it is not quite the thing for the dining room at home.

With approximately 35lb (16kg) per square inch of pressure at the cork it's a good idea to keep hold of it when you open the bottle and make sure you never aim it at anyone.

Make sure you have the glasses ready in case you do get a rush of foam when the bottle is opened. Stand the bottle on a sturdy surface and remove the foil from around the cork – there is usually a tab to pull. Grip the cork with your left hand. Using your right hand, bend the small wire ring that is normally folded up against the bottle downwards and unscrew it to loosen the wire cage from its grip on the cork. Spread this wire wide and away from the bottle. With the left hand still in position, thumb on cork top, rotate the bottle with your right hand a little to the left then a little to the right and repeat until you feel the cork start to rise. You are now in control of the cork's exit; gradually allow it to rise to the top of the bottle against your hand.

Once you feel the cork has made it to the top, angle the cork with your hand and left thumb, keeping the cork firmly in contact with the bottle top. Allow the pressure to escape from the tiny gap that you have made between the bottle and the cork, and let all of the pressure escape before you move your hand. If the bottle has been shaken there may be a rush of foam through the gap.

Note: Reverse these instructions if you are left handed.

Sabrage

If you are feeling particularly heroic or just want to show off perhaps the *Sabrage* method of opening a bottle of Champagne is for you. Made popular in Napoleonic France and still practised, *Sabrage* is the art of opening a bottle with a sabre. The bottle is held at arm's length and a sabre is run very quickly along and in contact with the bottle from bottom to top and literally smashes the top of the bottle off as the sabre makes contact with the band of glass at the neck and breaks it off just under the cork. It's theatrical and very wasteful but it is very entertaining. You will need a sabre, a dustpan and brush, a bucket of warm water and a mop.

Serving Champagne

Pour a small amount into the glass then stop pouring and wait for a few moments for the frothing to subside and continue to pour; the frothing is now reduced, which makes filling the glass easier and faster. Don't bother to tip the glass over as if you are pouring a bottle of light ale; it makes no difference to the foaming whatsoever.

If you are setting up glasses for a Champagne reception, pour a small amount of Champagne in each glass just before the first guests arrive – you can then fill glasses at a much faster rate, without causing the Champagne to foam over the glasses. Pour only two-thirds of a glass. The reason for this is simple: Champagne should be enjoyed chilled. If the glass is held for any length of time while the drink is sipped it will warm up and warm Champagne is horrible. So the smaller the amount the quicker it will be consumed and enjoyed cool.

Champagne should be served thoroughly cold but not icy and once opened the bottle should be left cooling in a Champagne bucket of ice and water. A full bottle is quite heavy so to avoid the risk of dropping it, hold it as you would any other bottle with one hand and support it under the neck with the fingers of the other.

Storing Champagne

A cellar is the best place. Store the bottle on its side, away from direct sunlight and the extremes in temperature fluctuation that can occur in the kitchen. Best storage temperature is about 13°C (55°F) or slightly lower. It is a myth that Champagne can be kept for years on end and that the longer it is kept the better it will be. For best results, keep it for no longer than three or four years. Chill in the refrigerator for only a couple of days before serving.

Should there be any left over the best way to keep it fresh is simply to keep the open bottle upright in the fridge. The effectiveness of the old 'silver spoon in the neck' trick to save the bubbles is a hard one to prove but there are some very good stoppers on the market designed specifically to keep Champagne fresh.

Wine

Opening wine

A foil cutter and a quality corkscrew make life easier
and properly cut foil looks neat and more professional.
If the bottle is of great value and has been stored for
some years gently clean around the neck before you
open it but do not wash the dust from the bottle as
this greatly adds to the drama of an historic wine when
served and shows everyone how long you've had it.

Serving wine

Red wine is best served at room temperature, about
18°C (64°F). White wine and rosé should be chilled
in the fridge for a couple of hours before serving at
around 8–10°C (46–50°F). Champagne and sparkling
wines should be chilled a little longer to about 6–8°C
(43–46°F). Champagne and some rosé should be
served icy cold.

Some light-bodied reds and some dryer sherry types
may also be served chilled.

Why decant?

You can open a bottle of red wine an hour or so before you intend to drink it or carefully pour into a clean decanter. You may decant for the following reasons:

- To start the oxidisation process by introducing air into the wine brings the flavour and character of the wine out.
- To warm a red wine so it is at room temperature when you are ready to drink it.
- To remove sediment, which is often found in an older wine. To do this, keep the bottle as level as possible to ensure that no sediment is transferred and stop pouring before the sediment, which is at the very bottom of the bottle, reaches the neck. Steady the bottle on the top of the decanter if you want to. I have seen people run wine through a paper coffee filter in an effort to remove sediment but this should be considered very much a last resort, mainly because of the chemicals that might be found in the paper.

Wines can have other faults but with the now-frequent use of screw caps and synthetic corks, a 'corked' wine is thankfully rare. The unmistakable musty, mushroom-like aroma of a 'corked' wine is caused by a chemical released during the cleaning process of natural cork. If a wine appears too brown or smells similar to sherry, it may be oxidised, possibly a result of incorrect handling, having been stored upright or exposed to too much light.

Matching wine with food

This can be difficult because tastes and trends change as fast as newspaper headlines and it can take years to become an expert. Some of the traditional ways, which became the 'rules' and are therefore considered correct, are no longer being adhered to. Some red wines are enjoyed slightly chilled, for example, straight from the fridge, a custom that only a few years ago would have had serious wine buffs frowning. White wine is enjoyed at virtually any time, as an aperitif as well as with lunch or dinner, although now, most people drink red wine at dinner regardless of the menu.

It would seem that pretty much anything goes and with the exception of curry, where only an ice-cold beer is good enough, the whole subject of wine and food is very much a case of personal taste. White wines would normally be served at lunch and red wines for dinner, but this is not a hard-and-fast rule. White wines generally accompany lighter foods such as chicken and shellfish. The heavier red wines suit foods such as dark roast meats and game. Rosé and gris, specialities in Southern France, are served extremely cold and are drunk at any time of the day, including with breakfast.

Champagne and sparkling wines are drunk as a pre-dinner drink and the sweeter ones such as a demi-sec are drunk with pudding or cake. Port, a strong fortified blend of wine and brandy, is enjoyed at the end of dinner and is usually served with a cheese course. Sweeter white wines, for example Sauternes or a dessert wine such as Beaumes-de-Venise, can be served with pudding.

A short wine-tasting course

1. Pour the wine into a suitable glass – a tulip-shaped wine glass would be perfect. Wine glasses typically have this enclosing shape to hold the aroma of the wine in the glass.

2. Swill the wine around the glass, then stop and watch as the wine runs back down into the glass and hangs on the sides in thin bands. These bands are known as legs, and indicate the characteristic of the wine. The sweeter the wine the more legs there will be; this is also indicative of a superior wine.

3. Hold the glass over a white surface such as a tablecloth and have a look at the colour. If the wine is bright and has a fresh colour then all is well but if it appears to be too dark it could be old or oxidised.

4. Put the glass to your nose to check how the wine smells. It should have a pleasant aroma; you will tell in an instant if it doesn't.

5. To taste the wine, drink a very small amount and let it drop around your mouth and under your tongue, gently suck in some air and through the wine, it should sound a bit like a gargle, this way you will release the true flavours. Drink it or discard it, it's up to you, and at a serious tasting you may be offered a bucket in which to deposit the mouthful.

Avoid the temptation to eat while you are doing this and avoid cheese, especially if you happen to be buying, because even the worst wines taste good with cheese. It used to be a trick that some wine merchants would pull, to save the poorest quality until last and serve it with cheese and, as the combination is so good, they hope you will buy.

Storing wine

Ideally wine should be stored in a cool, dark place with minimal temperature fluctuations and away from vibrations and strong odours. Bottles should be stored on their side in humid conditions to keep the cork moist and to prevent air from entering the bottle. The majority of inexpensive wine is intended to be consumed within six to twelve months, and reds within two years. Great wines can be kept for hundreds of years and some will improve. Storing wine in a kitchen is to be avoided. For longer-term storage if you don't have a cellar, purpose-designed wine fridges are available, which store bottles in perfect conditions.

Three sheets to the wind

The term sheets, as all sailors will know already, refers to ropes and not sails. In the days of square-rigged vessels there was one sheet at each corner of each sail to keep it in place. And fairly obviously, if some of them came off, the sail would just flap, or more correctly, flog about. With three sheets untied or loosened the sails became uncontrollable and the boat would lurch about in much the same way as a drunken sailor, so at a fairly advanced stage of inebriation the sailor was known to be 'three sheets to the wind', which is far more polite than some of the descriptions applied to the condition these days.

It is not funny and not a very comfortable situation for anyone having to be at the table or in the same room with a loud out-of-control drunk. The problem is that alcohol tends to have a habit of creeping up when you're not looking, so slow down if you don't want to be that person.

CHAMPAGNE AND SPARKLING WINE

Champagne was discovered accidentally by French monk Dom Pérignon (1638–1715), who found that bubbles formed as a result of an incomplete fermentation process, which stopped during the cooler months and resumed when the weather began to warm. At the time, the bubbles were considered the mark of bad wine-making, but after some experimentation with grape blends, Dom Pérignon realised that the resulting wine was actually quite pleasant – at least that's how the story goes.

The main two grapes used in sparkling wine are chardonnay and pinot noir. Sparkling wine can be made from each separately or both together. The terms 'Champagne' and 'sparkling wine' are often used interchangeably, but only those wines produced in the Champagne region of France (Epernay) are allowed to be called Champagne. Those made elsewhere are sparkling wines, although many are produced using *méthode champenoise*, the natural process that causes the bubbles rather than adding carbon dioxide artificially, and are labelled accordingly. Champagne is best drunk chilled and typically does not improve with age.

Types of sparkling wines and Champagnes

Blanc de Noir
Made from black pinot noir grapes, the skins are removed before the colour is extracted. The colour can vary from gold to bright pink, and Blanc de Noir is full-bodied.

Blanc de Blanc
Made entirely from white grapes usually the chardonnay and pinot gris; the result is light and fruity.

Extra Brut
Dry, containing less than 6g (¼oz) of sugar per litre (1¾ pints).

Brut
Dry, containing less than 15g (½oz) of sugar per litre (1¾ pints).

Extra sec or extra dry
Semi-sweet, containing 12–20g (around ¾oz) of sugar per litre (1¾ pints).

Sec
Sweet, containing 17–35g (¾–1¼oz) of sugar per litre (1¾ pints).

Demi-sec
Sweeter than Sec, containing 33–50g (1–1¾oz) of sugar per litre (1¾ pints).

Doux
Very sweet, containing more than 50g (1¾oz) of sugar per litre (1¾ pints).

Vintage and NV
Champagne made from one specific good year. A non-vintage (NV) is the signature Champagne of a producer and is made with a blend of wines from different years.

Prestige Cuvée
Champagne made from specially selected fruit.

Spumante
The Italian for sparkling: Asti Spumante is an example. Prosecco is a popular Italian sparkling wine.

Cava
A Spanish alternative to Champagne, and much cheaper.

AN ESSENTIAL
BAR GUIDE

GLASSES

You can pour a drink into virtually anything you want to but setting out the right glass is important, especially at the table, since it shows that you understand how to do things properly. There are hundreds of different shapes of glasses designed for nearly as many drinks and far too many to list. Just be sure they are immaculately clean and sparkle, and never breathe on them in order to polish away any last-minute marks (see page 30).

Beer glasses

The mug
The beer mug is the traditional beer glass with dimples and a handle, sometimes referred to as a jug or a Britannia pint; government stamped. These are now considered very old fashioned.

Nonic pint or sleever
The British straight beer glass is perfect for a Guinness. In Ireland you ask for a glass if you want a half. The nonic pint is the original straight pint glass with the slight broadening at the top; one pint government stamped. The half pint is the same shape.

It is known as a sleever in the West Country, which may sound strange but in the days of old ale houses it was possible to buy a cuff of ale, so presumably the glass or tankard at the time resembled a cuff, which might explain the term sleever.

Martique pilsner

This is the 300ml (10fl oz) traditional flared beer or lager glass.

Wine glasses

White-wine glass

This is a clear, thin-stemmed glass, with an elongated oval bowl tapering inwards at the rim. Typical size is 240ml (8fl oz).

Red-wine glass

These can vary in size enormously. This is a clear, thin-stemmed glass with a round bowl tapering inwards at the rim. Typical size is 375ml (13fl oz).

Champagne glasses

Champagne flute

This is tulip-shaped, long and thin although shapes and designs vary; designed to keep the bubbles as long as possible. Typical size is 180ml (6fl oz).

Champagne coupe

A lovely glass, the first is said to have been modelled from a cast of Marie Antoinette's breasts, which is probably nonsense, but still makes the glass fun to hold, naturally. Coupes are traditionally used to build Champagne fountains.

Other glasses for the bar

Brandy glass or snifter
The shape of this glass concentrates the alcoholic odours to the top of the glass as the hands warm the brandy. Typical size is 525ml (18fl oz).

Cocktail or Martini glass
This glass has a triangular bowl design with a long stem and is used for a lot of straight-up (no ice) cocktails including Martinis, Manhattans, Metropolitans and Gimlets. Typical size is up to 360ml (12.5fl oz).

Sherry glass
This is the preferred glass for aperitifs, ports and sherry. The copita, with its aroma-enhancing narrow taper, is a good example and holds about 60ml (2fl oz). In the UK there is also a stemmed, waisted glass; the larger of this variety is called a 'schooner'.

Shot glass
This is a small glass suitable for vodka, whisky and other shorts. Many 'shot' mixed drinks also call for shot glasses. Typical size is 45ml (1.5fl oz).

Highball glass
This straight-sided glass, like a tumbler, is an elegant way to serve a variety of drinks, such as a gin and tonic or a Bloody Mary. Typical size is 240–360ml (8–12.5fl oz). Use a smaller variety for water.

Margarita glass

Slightly larger and more rounded than a cocktail glass, with a broader rim for holding salt, this is an ideal glass for Margaritas, Daiquiris and other fruit drinks.

BAR TERMINOLOGY

Many of the terms and phrases listed below are standard throughout the industry. A good bar person will know what you mean if you ask for something by name.

Chaser: A mixer, drunk straight after any other alcoholic drink for a new taste.

Cocktail: Any mixture of any drinks served with fruit and served chilled.

Cup: A punch-type drink made in smaller quantities than those made in a punch bowl.

Lace: The last ingredient to be poured into the glass.

Fizz: An effervescent drink, i.e. made with carbonated drinks, or one that emits bubbles a bit like a Spritzer (white wine and soda water).

Grog: A rum-based drink with water, fruit juice and sugar, commonly served in a large mug.

Mulled: Sweetened wine or beer served warm or hot; the best example is glühwein.

Neat: Straight, unaccompanied alcohol.

Nightcap: A wine or alcoholic drink taken just before bedtime.

On the rocks and straight up: The first is any drink served with ice cubes; straight up is without.

Pick-me-up: A drink thought to relieve the after-effects of over-indulgence in alcohol. Also known as the hair of the dog (see page 146).

Punch: Party-sized drink of fruit, fruit juices, flavourings, sweeteners, wine and various spirits. Served from a ladle into glass cups.

Shooter or shot: A single shot of spirit.

Toddy: A sweetened drink served hot and often with spices, served in a tall glass.

Tot: A small measure of alcohol/spirit.

Virgin: A non-alcoholic drink, such as a Virgin Mary.

MIXING DRINKS

Shaking

When a drink contains eggs, fruit juices or cream,
it is necessary to shake the ingredients. Use a cocktail
shaker to mix ingredients together and chill them
simultaneously. The object is to almost freeze the drink
while breaking down and combining the ingredients.
Normally this is done with the mixer three-quarters full
of ice. When you have poured in the ingredients put the
lid on and, holding the two parts together, shake the
shaker vigorously. When you see water condensing on
the outside of the shaker it is time to pour the contents
through a strainer.

Straining

Most cocktail shakers are made with a built-in strainer
or a hawthorn strainer. When a drink calls for straining
make sure you use ice cubes as crushed ice can block
some strainers. If a drink is made and shaken with
crushed ice, it is not usually strained.

Muddling

To extract the most flavour from certain fresh ingredients
such as fruit or mint garnishes, you should crush the
ingredient with the muddler on the back end of your bar
spoon or with a pestle.

Stirring

You can stir cocktails well with a metal or glass rod in a mixing glass. Use ice cubes to prevent dilution and strain the contents into a glass when the surface of the mixing glass starts to collect condensation.

Flaming

Flaming is the method by which a cocktail or spirit is set alight, normally to enhance the flavour of the drink.

Some alcoholic drinks will ignite easily if their proof (or alcoholic content) is high. Heating a small amount of the drink in a spoon will cause the alcohol to rise to the top, which can be easily lit. This can then be poured over the prepared ingredients. Don't add alcohol to drinks that are already alight and don't leave them unattended; light them where they pose no danger to any guest and away from other flammable items. Always extinguish a flaming drink before offering it or drinking it.

DECORATING DRINKS

Decoration of a cocktail will normally consist of
one or two fruit, herb or cherry garnishes that either
complement the flavour of the drink, contrast with the
colour or both. It is important to avoid overpowering
the drink. When garnishing with a slice of fruit be
careful with the size; too thin is flimsy while too thick
can unbalance not just the look of the cocktail but
sometimes also the flavour.

Citrus twists

Cut a thin slice of the citrus fruit crosswise and simply
twist to serve on the side of a glass or in it. To make a
spiral of citrus peel, use a vegetable peeler to cut away
the skin, working in a circular motion. Take care not to
cut into the bitter pith. For citrus peel knots, use strips
of peel and carefully tie them into knots.

Cocktail sticks

Used for spearing pieces of fruit, olives and cherries.
They are not reusable and certainly not for cleaning
your teeth in public.

Frosting

Margaritas and other mixed drinks often call for the rim of the glass to be coated with sugar, salt or another powdered ingredient and this is known as frosting. Rub the rim of the glass with a slice of a citrus fruit then dip the very edge of the rim into a small bowl of the required powder.

Other essentials

You should always have a good supply of Maraschino cherries; they are the most widely used of all decorations in cocktails. Have a selection of green olives and silver onions for Martinis. Straws are essential for children's drinks and some cocktails.

You may also like to keep a selection of tiny paper umbrellas and sparklers, which are all slightly kitsch, but can be popular.

Tips for dealing with breakages

If you drop a glass, don't attempt to catch it,
let it fall.

If a glass is dropped and it breaks, use a dustpan and
brush to pick the bits up; don't use your fingers.

If you break a glass near the ice bucket, throw away
the ice and start again.

Never push a glass to move it, always pick it up and
place it where you want it. Avoid marking the bowl
or rim of the glass with fingerprints when handling
glasses. Lift stemmed glasses from under the bowl
for support.

Never use a glass as an ice scoop, as the cold can
cause glasses to shatter.

AFTERNOON TEA, COFFEE AND CHOCOLATE

TEA

Queen Victoria's lady in waiting, Anna, the seventh Duchess of Bedford, started the fashion for taking afternoon tea in the 1830s, apparently because she couldn't wait for dinner and so ordered 'a little something to see her through until supper time'. It wasn't long before the idea caught on and tea served with light sandwiches, biscuits, hot teacakes and scones became quite the 'in thing' across the British Empire.

As dinner was traditionally served at around 8pm in Victorian times the upper classes had afternoon or 'low' tea at around 4pm, whereas the middle and lower classes had 'high' tea at around 5.30 to 6pm in place of dinner, and this consisted of items such as meat pies or smoked fish and cakes. The 'high' and 'low' descriptions are derived from the height of the table from which the teas were taken; the 'high' referring to tea taken at a dining-room table and 'low' tea being taken from a table at about the height of a coffee table.

How one took one's tea soon became something of a social minefield. As only the most expensive bone china could cope with the relatively high temperature of the tea, those who could only afford cheaper pottery took

to pouring a small amount of milk into the cup first
to avoid the risk of a breakage. Those who considered
themselves to be slightly better off would frown on
anyone doing such a thing and would be openly annoyed
should anyone do it to them. Legend has it that the
expression 'miffed' refers to those who got a bit
upset if their Milk was put In First.

The first coffee house, which also sold tea, opened in
London in 1652 but it wasn't until London had been
ravaged by the plague that Londoners became partial to
a cup of tea. People asked for the new drink from China
because they knew that to make tea you had to boil the
water first.

It is estimated that the British drink around 156 million
cups of tea every day. The chimpanzees, known as the
'Tipps' family, advertised tea as long ago as 1956.
Nowadays the chimpanzee known as Monkey is
knitted in two colours and speaks.

At many of the grand old hotels, the tea menu resembles
a wine list. Claridge's, which was named London's top
tea place in 2006 by the UK Tea Council, serves more
than 30 types of tea including Royal White Silver Needles
tea, which is hand-picked at dawn on only two days of
the year.

The perfect cup of tea

It's not major science but it's worth getting it right. Use fresh, loose-leaved tea that has been stored at room temperature in an airtight container away from anything that is strongly flavoured or perfumed. Bring fresh water to the boil and pour a little into the teapot, swirl it around to warm the pot. Warming the pot ensures that the tea leaves infuse at the optimum temperature.

Measure the tea carefully using one rounded teaspoon of loose tea per cup to be served. Discard the water used for warming the pot, spoon in the loose tea and then, using water that is just off the boil, fill the teapot.

The brewing time is all important and depends on the variety of tea being served. The Tea Council recommends:

- Indian Darjeeling, two to three minutes
- Sri Lankan Ceylon Uva, three minutes
- Indian Assam and Sri Lankan Ceylon Dimbula, three to four minutes

Adding milk or a slice of lemon to any variety of tea is a matter of personal taste, as is whether you choose to add your milk to the cup before or after the tea. Twinings, the tea merchants, suggest that you put the milk in first. As a general rule you should add roughly 1½ teaspoons of, ideally, full-fat milk at room temperature to your cup and then pour the tea, through a strainer, into the teacup. Re-fill the teapot with enough hot water to make a second brew and keep the pot warm using a tea cosy.

If you are making tea in a mug with a teabag pour the boiling water on first then add the milk. If you do it the other way around the tea does not infuse the water in quite the same way.

A table setting for afternoon tea

A tea plate with a napkin placed on top, a small knife to the right of the tea plate, and a pastry fork to the left. To the right of the tea plate and slightly in front of the knife, place a cup and saucer with a teaspoon. Just out in front of the plate setting, closer to the middle of the table and between every second person, place a sugar box with tongs or a sugar spoon, a milk jug and a tea strainer.

Howzat! Cricket tea

For some it's the most important part of the cricket match – especially those who don't find the gentle 'thock' of leather on willow very exciting. But it's true that, in the cricketing world, the tea is considered a sacred part of the proceedings.

Favoured items for the modern tea at the weekend league level include sausages, crisps, sandwiches, homemade cakes, scones with jam and cream, jugs of squash and, of course, tea.

Cricket Tea Menu

Sandwiches
Cheese and tomato
Ham and English mustard
Egg mayonnaise
Tinned salmon and cucumber

Cakes
Homemade Victoria sponge
Homemade scones with strawberry jam
and clotted cream

Tea
Pots of good-quality black tea

The first Laws of Cricket were implemented in February 1774 when a group of gentlemen got together in the Star and Garter in Pall Mall to lay down a set of rules that have been followed by cricketers in England ever since. As to the question of when the twenty-minute tea interval, which is now an integral part of every Test Match, actually came about there is no answer. At Marylebone Cricket Club at Lord's cricket ground in London, commonly known as the MCC, I was told by the catering department that they still have a very traditional tea during games but without the cakes. They have energy bars instead, due to the strict diet of the players.

Devon clotted-cream tea

Is a scone a *scoan* as in Sloane or a *scon* as in Don? Do you put the jam on the scone first then the cream or the cream then the jam? The dispute goes on. Whatever you say or however you do it, it is still one of the best things to come out of the West Country.

A Classic Cream Tea

Two warm scones
Clotted cream
Strawberry jam
A pot of tea

COFFEE

There are a number of ways to brew roast and ground coffee; the most popular two are the cafetière and the filter method.

Always make sure your coffee maker and the coffee pot are clean. Choose the right grind of coffee for your coffee maker. Ideally medium-ground coffees should be used in cafetières and finely ground coffee used in filters and espresso machines.

Use fresh water to brew the coffee. Water makes up 98 per cent of a cup of coffee and its quality will affect the flavour of the brew.

When filling a cafetière allow one dessertspoon of coffee per cup. You may wish to adjust the quantity according to required taste.

Use 'just off the boil' water. Boiling water will scald your coffee and spoil the flavour. Serve coffee immediately to enjoy its full, rich flavour and aroma. To ensure your coffee stays fresh always use within three weeks of opening the packet and, after opening, make sure you reseal the pack and store it in an airtight container – some say in the refrigerator. Never bother re-heating coffee; the flavour is awful.

HOT CHOCOLATE

The history of hot chocolate goes back to the Central American Mayan civilisation some 1,500 years ago. They made a bitter-sweet drink from cacao beans, from the plant that thrived in the rainforests. It was fermented with maize and chilli.

The Mayans referred to it as *theobrama cacao* or 'food of the gods'. The Aztecs prized cacao so highly that it was used as currency and called it *xocoatl* or 'bitter water'. The Spanish conquistadors found this almost impossible to pronounce and just called it *chocolat*. Hernan Cortez is said to have been responsible for bringing chocolate to Spain in 1544. The Spanish then successfully hid the concoction from the rest of Europe for a century or so, but the cat was out of the bag by the 1700s. The English added milk to the mixture and an 'e' to the end of the word. Sources conflict as to exactly who first served it hot. There is another theory that the word comes from the Mayan *chocol haa*, which means 'hot water' so, who knows, it may have been them.

The fastest way to make hot chocolate is to add a few spoons of ready-mixed chocolate powder into warm milk then bring it almost to the boil and serve. There are some really good-quality powdered chocolate products on the market and some that are made up of tiny pellets of pure chocolate, which dissolve easily into hot milk. But you should spoon carefully with this variety because, although it gives a luxurious result, it is very strong – spoon especially carefully when giving it to children.

FOOD: THE LOGISTICS

ESTIMATING HOW MUCH FOOD YOU WILL NEED

Estimating the amount of food you will need for a party is one of the hardest parts of entertaining. Trying to decide how much food you will need can be difficult and there is unfortunately no foolproof formula, but with practice it can be done. However, be careful not to overdo it.

Don't put your guests off

It's perfectly acceptable for guests to serve themselves and pass serving dishes around the dinner table but if you are going to dish everything up in the kitchen and place it all on the table, do get the amount you actually give them right. There is nothing more off-putting than huge quantities of food piled up in bowls and serving plates.

Not everyone wants to eat or is capable of eating vast quantities of food at dinner and anyway, dinner is usually late in the evening, which is not the best time to consume very large amounts.

If too much is put in front of diners, guests can be so overwhelmed that they hardly eat at all. You don't have to put everything on the table at once; just keep some in the kitchen and simply offer more if you have to.

However, if the guests know there are going to be several courses, they actually eat very little. Everyone seems to be on a diet most of the time anyway and a lot of people are extremely conscious of what they are eating.

Many people consider a dinner party to be is more of a social gathering with food thrown in; it's not really a time to load your plate as if you are never going to eat again. A small amount at a time looks better anyway and if you're lucky you can always have more.

Size

If you are in any doubt at all make up a plate while you are preparing for the evening and just see if everything you have in mind to serve will actually fit and what it will look like on the plate. This way you can judge if it is going to be too much or possibly not enough; two small potatoes, about three to four small carrots, a piece or two of broccoli and the meat or fish. Try it, see what looks right, then add some more to the overall amount if you think it's not enough or reduce it and you will be about right. It's not an exact science, more a case of practice makes perfect.

When cooking rice allow three-quarters of a cup or slightly less per person (see page 92 for a foolproof recipe), while for pasta fill a white-wine glass per person with dried pasta or simply follow the per-person advice on the packet.

JD's perfect rice

Allow three-quarters of a cup of rice per person.

Wash the rice in a bowl of water just to be sure there are no unwanted bits and to wash off some of the starch. Then drain away the water.

Into a large saucepan measure the same amount of cold water as rice, that is to say three-quarters of a cup of water per person.

Pour in the rice in such a way as to create a peak just above the water; this is an indication that you have the right amount of water and the rice will not turn out soggy.

With the lid on the pan, bring to the boil, stir once after adding a pinch of salt and a knob of butter. Turn the heat right down to very low and with the lid on leave to cook for at least twenty minutes. Resist all temptation to stir the rice; just leave it to soften. Test a grain or two after twenty minutes and if necessary leave for a further five to ten minutes.

Lift some rice from the bottom of the pan to the top with a fork and check that the rice is soft by pinching a few grains between your index finger and your thumb.

SAFE PRACTICE WITH FOOD

Maintaining personal and kitchen hygiene are important and effective ways to stop germs from spreading.

Personal hygiene

Wash your hands and nails in hot, soapy water before handling food, between handling cooked and uncooked foods, and after going to the lavatory. Rinse your hands well and dry them on a clean hand towel. Use different cloths for different jobs like washing up and cleaning surfaces. Wipe down and disinfect surfaces and wash utensils regularly, using a detergent or a very dilute solution of bleach. Wash up using hot water and a washing-up liquid. Never handle or prepare food for anyone if you have stomach problems such as diarrhoea or vomiting or if you have a cold. Cover any cuts or skin damage on your hands with waterproof plasters and, if possible, remove rings, watches and bracelets before handling food; tie your hair back.

Kitchen hygiene

Allow leftover food to cool to room temperature before storing it in the fridge, ideally within two hours of preparation. If necessary, divide leftovers into smaller portions to help food cool more quickly. Use up leftovers within two days and remember that cooked rice should only be kept for one day.

Raw foods such as meat should be kept in airtight containers and at the bottom of the fridge to reduce the risk of blood or juices dripping on to other food.

Defrost frozen foods in the fridge. Place them on a plate or in a container so that as they defrost they don't drip on or contaminate other foods. Keep the fridge at less than 5°C (41°F) and the freezer at -18°C (-0.4°F) or below. Don't store opened tins of food in the fridge – transfer the contents to an airtight container instead.

If food isn't cooked at a high-enough temperature harmful bacteria will survive. Follow the recipe or the instructions on the packet for cooking times and temperatures. Pre-heat the oven properly when neccessary. Take special care that things like pork, sausages, burgers and poultry are cooked through and are not pink in the middle. Using a clean skewer, pierce meat towards the end of the suggested cooking time; when cooked properly the juices run clear. Beef and lamb joints can be cooked rare but must be thoroughly sealed, that is to say browned, on the outside.

When using a microwave open the door from time to time and give the food a quick stir to ensure even cooking; only re-heat food once and only serve when you are sure it is properly heated through. You can use a food thermometer to check core temperatures if you want to.

Ratings for cooking beef and lamb
The ratings given opposite are generally applied to beef, lamb and minced meat, such as hamburger mince.

Rare	Centre is bright red, pinkish towards the outside
Medium rare	Centre is very pink but slightly brown towards the outside
Medium	Centre is light pink, outside is brown
Medium/well done	No longer pink
Well done	Uniformly brown throughout

If you happen to be dining somewhere that refers to the cooking of steak in French, the following chart may be useful.

Bleu	Placed on a very hot grill for 1 minute on each side
Saignant	Means bloody and very rare but cooked slightly longer on the second side than '*bleu*'
A point	Rare by British standards but cooked a little longer than '*saignant*'
Bien cuit	Cooked until the juices run brown on the surface of the steak.
Très bien cuit	A steak that is totally cooked through

How to sharpen a knife using a steel

A blunt knife is pointless, very frustrating and very dangerous. Some chefs maintain that you will never cut yourself with a sharp knife. Mechanical knife sharpeners, manual or electric, can rapidly and unevenly wear away the edge of a blade, so the best way – and the secret of keeping a keen edge on a knife – is frequent sharpening using a steel. Getting to grips with this requires a little practice but it is simple to do.

- Hold the knife in the right hand (if right handed) and the steel in the other hand.
- Keep the knife at a constant 20-degree angle against the steel and draw the blade across and down the steel with a medium pressure until the tip of the blade is near the handle of the steel.

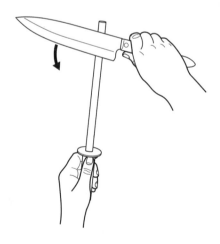

- Repeat the process on the other side of the blade and continue until the knife is sharp.

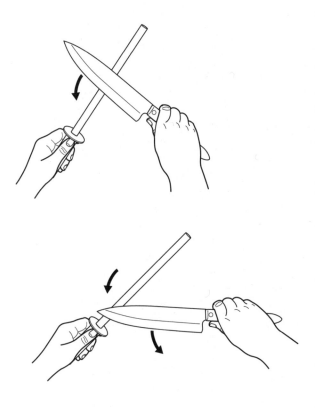

- Sharpness can be judged by drawing the blade across a sheet of writing paper; when properly sharp the knife will cut through the paper as if through butter.

THE COCKTAIL
PARTY

Organising a cocktail party or a reception doesn't need to be complicated. Depending on the formality of your event, send out invitations in good time, have enough to eat for the amount of people invited and a good selection of drinks that you know your guests will enjoy.

Canapés

Basically canapés are one-bite, mouth-sized finger food and are perfect for a cocktail party, but if that is all you are serving they should be good quality, plentiful and as attractive as possible. Canapés are the same as *hors d'oeuvres* and are usually made with a base of bread or crackers topped with small savouries. Another, more elaborate term sometimes applied to canapés is the so-called *amuse-bouche*; these are an assortment of canapés made up of numerous flavours for the guests to 'amuse the tastebuds'. All are typically served before dining, with drinks or when there could be a wait before dinner or they can be served as a stand-alone main course in the case of a cocktail party or a reception.

Although they can sometimes look the same, canapés should not be confused with petit fours, which can be sweet or sometimes savoury, and which are served at the end of dinner.

Petit fours

As 'four' is the French word for oven, strictly speaking petit fours are very small oven-baked cakes, but can also be biscuits. Classically made with choux or flan pastry they are generally sweet, although savoury recipes do exist. Some varieties are not necessarily cooked but instead made with bases like meringue or marzipan.

SOME CLASSIC COCKTAILS

Cocktail fashions change fast, and often the 'in thing' doesn't last long. So although you may be up to speed with what is currently 'in', unless you are a professional bartender you can't really be expected to know everything. Listed on the following pages are a few old classics but if you want to get into making cocktails in a big way you will need some sort of guide and one that's a lot more comprehensive than this. I make it a habit of travelling with a pocket guide in the hope that I won't be caught out by a request.

Bloody Mary

A cocktail and a pick-me-up, enjoyed before dinner and lunch, sometimes as a morning-after tonic and a fine mixture for some people to help appease the after-effects of the excesses of the night before.

A Bloody Mary has many variations. This recipe is about as close as it gets to the original, which was formally known as a Red Snapper and was first mixed by bartenders at the St Regis Hotel in New York in 1934.

30–34ml (1–1¼1fl oz) vodka in a highball glass
Add a cube or two of ice
Top up with tomato juice
1 dash of celery salt
1 dash of ground black pepper
1 dash of Tabasco
2–4 dashes of Lea and Perrin's Worcester sauce
¹/₈ tsp horseradish, pure, not creamed
Squeeze of lemon or lime juice

May be shaken vigorously or gently stirred as desired. Garnish with a celery stalk, a skewer of olives, pickles, carrots, mushrooms or other vegetables. Sometimes salami, prawns or cheese and occasionally asparagus or beans are used, and some people like to add a measure or two of fino sherry, for the flavour. The alcohol-free version is known as a Virgin Mary.

Another famous restorative is the Bullshot, which is cold beef bouillon and vodka.

Champagne cocktail

Along with adding Champagne to Guinness for a Black Velvet, this is one of the only times when I think it's just about acceptable to mix Champagne with something else and this mixture is a good one: a couple of these and your party will definitely go well.

4 drops of Angostura Bitters
1 sugar cube
0.75 shot of Cognac
Champagne

Drip the Angostura Bitters on to the sugar cube and place in the bottom of a Champagne flute. Cover the cube with Cognac. Top up with Champagne.

Vodka and tonic

There are those who insist that the addition of tonic water ruins vodka, but then if you left the tonic out altogether it would just be neat vodka. Nothing really comes close to the sharpness, the clarity and the power of this standard cocktail.

Pour two measures of vodka over a couple of ice cubes in a highball glass. Drop a slice of lemon into the glass. Leave for while to chill the spirit then top with about the same amount of fresh tonic water. Do the same thing but with gin for a gin and tonic (see page 104).

Gin and tonic

A classic that has been with us for over 150 years, which was first put together as an anti-malaria concoction in colonial India. Quinine was added to carbonated water to give Indian tonic; the quinine being the anti-malaria 'tonic', which was then mixed with gin to make it more appealing.

Gin

Gin originated in Holland in about 1550 when a professor of medicine Franciscus de la Boe was trying to find a cure for stomach ailments using the diuretic properties of juniper berries and stumbled on this wonderful infusion, which he named Genever. It soon became popular as an alcoholic drink. Gin came back to Britain with troops returning home from the Thirty Years' War where they had been given rations of gin to keep out the cold before battle and from then on it was referred to as 'Dutch courage'. The spirit is from a base of either grain or molasses and has no flavour. The flavouring comes from botanicals but all gins include juniper. Other ingredients such as angelica, cardamom, coriander and lemon can be added and nearly all recipes differ from producer to producer, and are regarded as being very much of a trade secret.

Martini cocktails

Drip a few drops of Angostura Bitters around the inside of a martini glass, pour in very chilled gin and add a green olive on a cocktail stick; this almost amounts to the once medicinal British naval concoction known as Pink Gin, but in this case don't drip enough to really colour the drink. Add a silver onion instead of the olive and you have a Gibson Martini. There are many different variations and not everyone would agree with this one but in common with quite a few bartenders I like the idea of a Martini sans everything.

Martini

Martini and Rossi created Martini Rosso, a dry vermouth in 1863, and it is thought that an American bartender may have mixed gin with it and simply called it a Martini but the evidence is scarce. Others have it that it was invented by a bartender whose name was Martini at the Knickerbocker Hotel in New York for John D. Rockefeller in 1910 and made with French vermouth. W. Somerset Maugham said that 'Martinis should always be stirred, not shaken, so that the molecules lie sensuously one on top of the other', whereas Ian Fleming's James Bond prefers a Vodka Martini famously 'shaken not stirred', which, to be correct, should be called a Bradford. Apparently recent medical research has shown that shaken Martinis have a slightly higher antioxidant level than those stirred.

The Classic American Martini

55ml (2fl oz) gin
15ml (¼ tsp) vermouth
Ice cubes
Green olive
Lemon peel

Pour the gin and the vermouth into a cocktail shaker
with ice cubes and shake. Strain into a chilled Martini
cocktail glass. Squeeze oil from lemon peel on to the
drink and garnish with an olive on a cocktail stick.

Vermouth

Created in the late 18th century and originally used
as a tonic because of the healing herbs in the recipe,
including wormwood, nutmeg, coriander, juniper,
orange peel, cloves, marjoram and cinnamon. The
name vermouth comes from the German word for
wormwood, *wermut*, pronounced 'vair-moot'.

Margarita

30–60ml (1–2fl oz) Tequila
15ml (½fl oz) Cointreau
Juice of ½ a lime

Shake well with ice or use a blender then strain into
martini glasses that have had the rim dipped in salt.

MOCKTAILS

For those that like the idea of a cocktail but don't want the alcohol, a 'mocktail' could be the answer. Famous versions include a Shirley Temple (given below) and the classic Virgin Mary (see page 102). The Not So Cosmo is really the same as a Cosmopolitan but without the vodka.

Not So Cosmo

25ml (1fl oz) freshly squeezed orange juice
25ml (1fl oz) cranberry juice
25ml (1fl oz) freshly squeezed lime juice
25ml (1fl oz) lemon juice
1 tablespoon sugar syrup

Shake all the ingredients together with ice and strain into a martini glass. Garnish with an orange zest twist.

Classic Shirley Temple

85ml (3fl oz) lime juice
85ml (3fl oz) ginger ale or lemonade
Dash of grenadine, to colour

Mix all the ingredients together in a cocktail shaker with some ice and shake. Pour into martini or highball glasses with some crushed ice. Decorate with a maraschino cherry and add a straw.

THE DINNER PARTY

Plan ahead. A formal dinner party shouldn't be a last-minute decision. Prepare a guest list in advance and choose guests who you think will enjoy each other's company, then send out invitations as soon as possible and including an RSVP (see page 19).

THE BEGINNING OF THE EVENING

I have already mentioned the old cliché that says we eat with our eyes and although obviously it is not meant literally, it's true – we only ever eat and drink what is immediately appealing and either subconsciously or physically discard the rest. To a certain extent we rate our surroundings in a similar way, so have a tidy up before your guests arrive. Prepare as much as possible beforehand (see page 12) and keep it simple: the less complicated the menu the better. This will go some way towards keeping your stress levels to a minimum and give you time to meet and greet your guests properly.

Handing plates of canapés around or topping up glasses is a chance to offer initial hospitality and make contact with your guests.

The importance of the first drink, the food, the decorations and the lighting should not be underestimated. Nothing adds to the atmosphere quite like the right music but not overpoweringly loud. Plan a style to suit the crowd and let your iPod do the rest. And don't forget there is nearly always someone who will fancy a dance. Lighting is crucial and candlelight never fails to set a romantic or dramatic scene.

Put away anything that you feel is private and that you don't want your guests to see or touch. This is especially important if any of your guests are children. Shut doors or lock rooms that are off limits and make sure the bathrooms are spotless.

There is no harm in sticking to tried-and-tested recipes; things you can prepare in advance such as soups, pies or casseroles. Of course, what you serve will largely if not completely depend on the likes and dislikes of the guests and to an extent on your available budget. One thing is absolutely for sure, whatever you decide to serve, three or four good-quality, well-prepared dishes made with high-quality ingredients are infinitely better than a dozen made from the opposite.

Be careful not to do a complete copy of your last party unless you have a menu that you know works well and your guests are different; something an Italian business acquaintance refers to as '*Stesso menu, diversi ospiti*', same menu, different guests.

Respect religion, vegetarians and anyone with food intolerances or allergies. If you are not sure and think that you might have a vegetarian coming, cook an option for them – if it is the case that none turn up, everyone else will eat it anyway.

Serve the guest or guests of honour first if you want to, if it's that kind of party, and although it is slightly old fashioned, you should really serve the ladies and older people first. Your seat should be nearest to the kitchen so that you can get out and tend to things without having to disturb any of the guests.

The main course should follow a starter quickly and hot foods must always be served on hot plates! Virtually every dinner guest will touch a dinner plate to see if it's warm and some are disappointed if it is not.

You can leave a longer gap before pudding and don't be in too much of a hurry to take plates away but offer second or even third helpings. You shouldn't remove anything from the table before everyone present has finished eating.

A QUICK DINNER PARTY MENU

On arrival

Offer a glass of Champagne or very cold brut cava for everyone on arrival and, as an alternative, have a few cold bottles of beer, such as Spitfire from Shepherd Neame, Britain's oldest brewery.

Cava

A Spanish alternative to Champagne at a fraction of the price; when properly chilled most people would be hard pushed to tell the difference. Easy to find in the supermarket too — just look for the empty section in the wine aisles.

Simple canapés

Use thin slices of the best smoked salmon you can afford and some faux caviar (see pae 114). Carefully place on separate pieces of toast, cut into uniform small squares and arrange on large serving plates. Slice spears of lightly steamed asparagus in half and add them to the salmon toasts for a green touch. Squeeze over some lemon juice at the last minute.

Caviar

The unfertilised roe of the female sturgeon, a fish from the *Acipenseridae* family. There are 24 existing sturgeon species worldwide, five of which live in the Caspian Sea and only three supply caviar; these are the beluga, the osetra and the sevruga. Prized as a delicacy for centuries, it rates as one of the world's most coveted delicacies and is very expensive. For the beluga sturgeon to reach a maturity sufficient to produce roe it takes approximately twenty years. Caviar was thought in the 19th century to 'hasten sexual desire and to excite the blood'. This is a claim that has never been proven but it is known that the eggs slow down the absorption of alcohol, allowing more vodka or Champagne consumption.

Caviar is served in small glass or porcelain dishes or in special servers on a bed of crushed ice, and sometimes in the original tin.

Don't take too much at a time: about a spoonful is about right. Serving spoons should be mother of pearl or horn as some metals taint the flavour. The best beluga should be eaten with toast points or simply on its own. One traditional Russian recipe is to eat it on blini, which are wholemeal pancakes.

Faux caviar: Looks the same as some genuine caviar but it comes from an entirely different fish and is a lot cheaper.

A starter

This is such a good soup that you only need to serve a very small amount.

Blender Soup with Curly Toast

1 glass of dry white wine
3 sticks of fresh celery
1 small onion
3 large carrots
1 or 2 small potatoes
2 rashers of smoked streaky bacon

Boil all the ingredients slowly in a small amount of water.

Drain off but keep the cooking water, then ladle the mixture into a blender and whizz until you have a fine, smooth, creamy consistency. Add sea salt and black pepper and some of the cooking water to thin the mix as you go, if you need to.

Ladle into soup bowls and add a dessertspoon of single cream and a dash of dry sherry. Float some fresh, roughly chopped coriander on to the soup.

Grill thick-sliced white bread on both sides. Cut off the edges of each slice to create a perfect square, then cut through the slice between the toasted faces. Put back under the grill and toast the sides that are not yet toasted; the result is wonderful curly toast. Serves with the soup.

Followed by...

Rocket, Mâche and Beetroot Salad

Arrange the thinnest slices of boiled (not pickled) beetroot on a plate and lightly cover with fresh, well-washed rocket and fastidiously well-washed mâche (lamb's lettuce, or corn salad in the US). Drizzle with a very small amount of your favourite salad dressing. Simple but looks great and is very good. Place it on the table after the soup.

Charred Poussin with Lemon

Pre-heat the oven to 225°C/425°F/gas mark 7.

Cut the poussin in half lengthways and trim away any unwanted bits of skin and the parson's nose; give it a good wash. You can use small chickens instead if you want to. Boil in chicken bouillon until just cooked through and then drain. Keep some of the boullion to thicken, for a sauce. Place the chicken on an oven tray skin side up and slide into the pre-heated oven, then turn the oven up to the highest setting. Leave them in until the skin is almost burnt; probably about five minutes or possibly a bit longer. Remove from the oven and arrange on a serving plate skin side up. Squeeze over fresh lemon juice and scatter on some chopped broad-leaved parsley. Serve immediately with roast potatoes.

Clifton Roast Potatoes

First perfected in Clifton, Bristol, in the 1980s.

Pre-heat the oven to 225°C/425°F/gas mark 7. Cut some new potatoes into quarters or in half depending on the size. Whether you peel them or not is entirely up to you.

Place the cut potatoes in a saucepan and cover with very slightly salted water. Boil gently until just at the parboiled stage. Drain and add a small amount of butter – about four or five pieces the size of a sugar cube – and a dessertspoon of virgin olive oil. Put the lid on the saucepan and shake until each piece of potato is lightly oiled. Tip the potatoes on to a baking tray and slide into the oven. Roast until golden brown. Open the oven for a few minutes before they are done and throw over some small sprigs of fresh rosemary (do this too early and the herb burns, leaving very indigestible hard bits). Grind on some black pepper and a little salt and serve in a large serving bowl.

Drink

Serve freezing-cold lightweight, Italian dry white wine or dry French rosé or, if you can afford it, another bottle of chilled Champagne – brut cava if you can't. Have carbonated cold English mineral water on the table for everyone to share.

A nice pear for dessert

The British climate of cold winters and gentle summers makes our pears some of the sweetest on the planet and I love them. This pudding is a tried-and-tested winner.

Peel one conference pear per person and cut in half from top to bottom so that one piece still has the stalk in place. Use a teaspoon to scoop out the core. Place in a large saucepan and cover with water. Add a couple of teaspoons of Demerara sugar and ¼ teaspoon of vanilla essence. Gently poach until soft. Halfway through pour in a glass of dry red wine and continue to poach until ready. If you cook for long enough the liquid will reduce to fabulous syrup. Serve warm with a dessertspoon of vanilla blancmange and some of the syrup.

Blancmange

Blancmange is an almost forgotten and old-fashioned pudding, one that probably brings back fond memories to 1960s schoolchildren. This recipe is great and nothing like the ones I endured. When I make it, I pour it into an old bent mould shaped like a sandcastle that I bought in a flea market. Every time I do it everyone loves it.

90g (3oz) cornflour
1.2l (2 pints) milk
115g (4oz) granulated sugar
30g (1oz) butter
1tsp vanilla essence
1 leaf of gelatine

Blend the cornflour in a saucepan with some of the cold milk. Then add in the rest of the milk, sugar and gelatine. Bring slowly to the boil over low heat, stirring from time to time. Once boiled, remove from the heat, add the butter and vanilla and stir together gently. Pour into a wetted mould and refrigerate. Turn out on to a serving plate once properly set and completely cold.

Afterwards, coffee is a must as are bars of chocolate.

FORMAL DINING, GRACES AND TOASTS

Often steeped in tradition and rituals, formal dinners are still commonplace in the Royal Navy, at some universities and at the Inns of Court. For the uninitiated they can be mystifying affairs. It is the responsibility of the person who invited you, if you need help, to guide you and explain what to expect and how to behave. In the case of a Forces dinner, for example, the ladies are required to have their shoulders covered and should never eat with their gloves on (actually ladies should never do this anyway).

This is the time when your knowledge of correct form should kick in. Your table manners should be impeccable; keep an eye on the top table if you are still unsure how to proceed and in particular watch for signs as to when to sit down, start eating and leave the table. The top table should take their seats last. You should not leave the table during dinner. Be prepared to hear grace, speeches and in some cases, toasts.

SAYING GRACE

It is not only at formal events that many people observe the tradition of pausing before eating to give thanks for the food on their tables. When entertaining, unless your religion has a specific guideline, you can say whatever you like. You might like to copy the grace said in Latin at Oxford University:

Benedic, Domine, nos et donna tua quae de largitate tua
sumus sumpturi et concede, ut illis salubritter nutriti
tibi debitum obsequium, praestare valeamus, per
Christum Dominum nostrum.

(Bless O Lord us and your gifts which from your bounty
we are about to receive and grant that healthily
nourished by them we may render you due obedience
through Christ our Lord.)

And if that's too much it is often shortened to:

Benedic, Domine, donna tua quae de largitate sumpturi.

It is recommended that you finish with 'Amen'. It is
a prayer after all. Everyone will recognise it and will
know that you have finished.

TOAST ETIQUETTE

The first toast should be given by the host of the event.
For example, at a wedding reception, etiquette dictates
that the bride's father gives the first toast. It is extremely
bad manners for the person giving the toast to be even
slightly drunk, so if you are the speaker, save the drinking
for afterwards.

When giving a toast, start by stating how honoured you
are to have been asked to give the toast. Do not under
any circumstances use foul language, inappropriate

innuendo or even slang anywhere in the speech. Stand with your glass raised to get everyone's attention. You should not tap on your glass with a piece of cutlery. Do not start to speak until everyone is looking at you and the room is quiet. Ask everyone to stand with you to toast either the recipient or the occasion.

The toast speech is generally short and to the point. At the closing, hold your glass higher and face the entire group to propose the toast. Finally, conclude with whatever wishes you want to convey and any offers of congratulations that may be appropriate to the occasion.

When the toast is finished, it is proper for the recipient of the toast to stand, without drinking, and say a few words also.

Your glass should be about two-thirds full or at least have something in it to drink because it is considered bad toast etiquette to toast with an empty glass.

Don't raise your glass or drink from it until the speaker asks everyone to stand or raise a glass and it is not necessary to 'clink' glasses with anyone else – it's not done. It is never a good idea not to participate in a toast; if you are present at the event, you should participate in any toasts given. Alcohol is the traditional drink used for toasts, but any drink will do, and it's never good manners to applaud; you are already showing your agreement with your actions.

Why a toast?

Apparently a toast is called a toast because in the 17th century they used to raise a glass with a drink flavoured with spiced toast. The only reason it is thought wrong to 'clink' glasses during a toast is because when doing so there is a risk that you may spill your drink on to the clothes of someone else.

The Loyal Toast

At a very formal dinner it is possible for the National Anthem to be played followed by the Loyal Toast. If the National Anthem is played you should stand up, without speaking and leave your glass on the table until the end, when the toast may be offered.

The Loyal Toast is a toast to the monarch and the only one the Queen approves is simply 'The Queen'. The principal host would normally stand and say 'The Queen', then raise his glass and then the assembled, also standing, will raise their glasses and say after the host 'The Queen' and then drink a toast, again without 'clinking' glasses with anyone else. Speeches, smoking and port follow the toast.

SPEECHES

Although they can be desperately boring or just terrible, during the speeches good etiquette says that you should at least stay awake, be attentive and laugh in the right places and, although often almost impossible, you should try to avoid any audible sniggering. At a traditional wedding probably about five minutes is long enough if you are giving the speech. Inebriation at this stage or making any uncalled-for comments or inappropriate references will not go down well and this really is not the time or the place. Wedding speeches should be made in this order.

- The bride's father proposes a toast to the bride and groom and then talks about his daughter.
- The groom then responds on behalf of his wife. If at this point the groom takes the opportunity to refer to 'my wife and I', it can and often does generate a round of applause. The groom thanks everyone who has helped to organise the day then presents his and the bride's mother with a bouquet of flowers.
- He then thanks his attendants and presents them with gifts, speaks about his new wife and then proposes a toast to the bridesmaids.
- The best man then responds on behalf of the bridesmaids followed by any emails or cards from absentees. He then talks about the groom.

THE PORT RITUAL

The end of the Loyal Toast is when the speeches start and the port is brought to the table. Tradition states that a decanter of port is placed on the table for the host to pour a glass for himself, then for the person seated on his left. The decanter is passed to his left for the next person to do likewise. Be sure to pass it only to the left and never ever to the right. When pouring, the decanter must not be picked up from the table until the last glass is charged. If for some reason you missed it as it went past, you may not ask for it to be passed back but you should wait for it to go round again.

Smoking

Not so long ago no social occasion was complete without cigarettes and you could smoke inside public places too. Nowadays the smokers are very much in the minority.

As smoking is seen as a hazardous pursuit and the fumes highly toxic, consideration for non-smokers should be observed. If you must smoke, don't do it at the table and don't puff away in front of children and pregnant women. Always use a proper ashtray if you are allowed to smoke indoors, never a wine bottle, a plant pot or, worst of all, a used plate. Don't speak to anyone and exhale smoke at the same time or stand talking with a cigarette stuck in your mouth so that you have to tilt your head over to one side and then close an eye to avoid the smoke as if tying your shoelaces and smoking at the same time.

THE BURNS SUPPER

A Burns Supper is a celebration of the life and works
of the poet Robert Burns, author of many Scots poems
including 'Auld Lang Syne'. The suppers are held on
or near the poet's birthday, which is 25th January and
sometimes referred to as Burns Night, although in
principle they may be held at any time of the year.

Burns Suppers are most common in Scotland, but they
occur wherever there are Burns clubs, Scottish societies,
expatriate Scots or lovers of Burns's poetry. They may be
formal or informal but they are always entertaining. The
only items the informal suppers have in common are
haggis, Scotch whisky and perhaps a poem or two.

Order of the Burns Supper

At the start of the evening the guests gather and mix in
an informal way as at any other type of party. The host
then makes a welcoming speech and the event is declared
open. Everyone is seated at the tables and the host says
the Selkirk Grace:

Some hae meat and canna eat,
And some wad eat that want it;
But we hae meat, and we can eat,
Sea the Lord be thankit.

The supper then starts with a Scottish soup such as Scotch broth, potato soup or Cock-a-Leekie.

Entrance of the haggis

The haggis follows as the main course and everyone stands as it is brought in by the chef accompanied by a bagpiper. The haggis is laid in front of the host who then recites the 'Address to a Haggis', which has eight verses. At the line 'An' cut you up wi ready slicht' the host plunges the knife into the haggis and cuts it open from end to end. At the end of the poem, a whisky toast will be proposed to the haggis.

Haggis

A meat dish reminiscent of a large oval sausage, made by stuffing a sheep or cow stomach with offal, oatmeal and an assortment of spices and then boiling it. Although inextricably linked with Scottish culture, versions of the same thing can be found in other cultures and it is thought that the Romans may have brought it to Britain.

The supper

The main course is the haggis, traditionally served with 'tatties and neeps' or potatoes and swede (in the US, rutabaga or turnip). Pudding would probably be something like Cranachan or Tipsy Laird (sherry trifle), sometimes followed by oatcakes and cheese, with liberal tots of '*uisge beatha*' (water of life), better known as whisky. When the supper reaches the coffee stage various speeches and toasts are given, to the health of the monarch, the immortal memory of Burns, the 'lassies' and the 'laddies' present, and often to Scotland. Then there may be singing of songs and recitals of poetry by Burns, including 'To a Mouse' and 'To a Louse'.

Cranachan

Made with cream, Scottish heather honey, oatmeal, whisky and raspberries and served chilled or sometimes frozen.

Finally the host will wind things up, calling on one of the guests to give the vote of thanks, after which everyone is asked to stand, join hands and sing 'Auld Lang Syne'.

VOTE OF THANKS

The vote of thanks is an expression of appreciation to a speaker or event provider given by the recipient. It can be a nerve-wracking thing for some people to be asked to do at the last minute but it's a nice gesture and actually very straightforward, and should be kept short, simple and succinct. The opening sentence, once you have everyone's attention, might be as follows:

'Ladies and gentlemen, on behalf of us all I would like to thank Mr Smith for his speech and for an excellent lunch and I would like to ask the audience to express their appreciation in the usual way.'

A round of applause from the audience follows, which brings the event to a close.

EATING OUTSIDE

A BARBECUE

An outdoor party is a great excuse for some serious entertaining and a barbecue is an event that almost everyone enjoys, especially if the weather is good. There is without doubt a certain *je ne sais quoi* about chilled wine, charred meat and coleslaw out of doors.

Before you start your shopping check whether you have any vegetarians coming or anyone with allergies. Make sure you have plenty of food in reserve for any stragglers and late arrivals, and remember that the grilling tends to go on for several hours.

It's a strange phenomenon, the barbecue, because it seems to prompt otherwise reluctant cooks into action, to don a pinny and take up their tongs. But then, it really is only a case of turning things over. The key though, as with all cooking, is getting the timing right and being absolutely sure the food is properly cooked. Only start cooking when the charcoals are glowing red with a layer of grey ash, and move the food around the grill.

Chicken is one of the most sensitive foods to have at a barbecue, so rather than waiting three-quarters of an hour for a piece to cook over the flames and, to avoid it being thoroughly burnt on the outside and raw on the inside, boil it first before it goes on the grill, then you can be sure that by the time the outside has burnt to a crisp the inside is cooked and, more importantly, there is no chance of your guests going home with salmonella.

Marinade fresh meats yourself and avoid those pre-packed brightly stained offerings that appear on the supermarket chilled shelves during the *al fresco* grilling season. That way you know exactly what you have and the quality of the meat beneath.

Don't leave party foods that normally need to be chilled at room temperature for hours, but serve small amounts at a time and keep the rest in the fridge. Keep all serving bowls covered until the last minute.

Outwit any sudden changes in the fickle summer weather by having the house ready in case everyone has to retreat because of a downpour. Cook some things in the oven as well, so that should the barometer drop and conditions take a turn for the worse you have ready-cooked food – if they don't you can serve the dishes outside anyway.

Consider using unbreakable or disposable plates, paper napkins and some alternative to glass, especially if there are children coming and, more importantly, if your party is around a swimming pool. As with all outdoor activities involving food, be aware of insects and domestic pets; burn citronella candles to keep the gnats at bay in the evening and in common with anything to do with fires, make it a rule that only one person lights and attends to the barbecue and that any young children are kept at a safe distance.

THE MOVEABLE FEAST

Although the term was first coined by the French, the picnic is thought of as being about as quintessentially British as Ascot.

A good picnic is not just about the food; it's also about decent weather, so if you happen to be taking your hamper to some pre-paid ticket affair take an umbrella and a plastic-backed rug or some sort of groundsheet to sit on. Struggling to balance a fork and a glass while at the same time sitting on uneven ground can be awkward, so keep the menu simple. Sandwiches are an obvious choice but fillings that travel well are few and far between, so stick to things like ham and mustard or chicken in mayonnaise. Pork pies are an option as are Cornish pasties, some salads, together with a good cake and a flask for the all-important coffee. For anything more ambitious, such as picnicking at the races or if you happen to be formally dressed, a table and chairs are essential as are substantial knives and forks, real glasses and cloth napkins. Whatever you do, don't forget the bottle opener and the corkscrew. And remember, just because you are in a field it doesn't mean you can forget your table manners either.

Don't let anything hamper your day

Carry a pack of wipes to clean your hands and always wash your hands before preparing food and eating. If you have children with you, wipe their sticky fingers too.

Most foods need to be eaten fairly soon after leaving the fridge. Some foods travel well and some do not. If you are travelling far for a picnic you will need a coolbox and some ice packs. If you don't have ice packs, freeze some water in plastic bottles or make ice in the usual way and take a bag of it – then you will also have some ice cubes for drinks.

Leave everything you have prepared in the fridge until the last minute then, along with your ice, pack it into the coolbox.

Once out, keep your food covered as much as possible but if you think that your food has been in the sun for too long, throw it away. Protect it from insects, birds and pets, as all can carry bacteria. Watch out for wasps, which can be very sneaky. On a windy beach cover up and put a lid on the Tupperware where possible, because there is nothing like grit in the sandwiches to spoil things. Beware the hungry gull: they are forever starving and can be aggressive if they think they are entitled to a share of the goodies. A herring gull is quite capable of removing a whole roast chicken from a picnic basket while the owner isn't looking or stealing fish and chips from unsuspecting tourists at the seaside.

Carry refuse bags to collect up your rubbish and, to repeat a cliché, leave only footprints behind when you go. If you have picnicked or grilled on a beach don't leave your disposable barbecue behind along with empty cans and broken bottles. Don't bury your rubbish on the beach – it is not a landfill site.

For the cash rich and time poor, between the months of May and August the Lanesborough Hotel in Knightsbridge, London offers an organised picnic in Hyde Park. Advertised as the 'ultimate hassle-free picnic', it not only comes with crystal glasses, fine china and food prepared in the hotel kitchens but also a butler, which is about all you need for truly five-star lazy London lunch, apart from some sunshine.

EATING ON THE HOOF

During the working day, in a perfect world, we would
all be allowed the time to sit down and eat lunch or
dinner at a table or even on our laps. Unfortunately
in our culture, unlike in Central and Southern Europe
where the lunch break is sacrosanct, we have no option
at times but to eat on the go, even though doing so has
always been rather frowned upon. Eating in the street,
it would seem, is only acceptable if you sit down
somewhere to do it. At lunchtime, when the sun is out,
London parks are a perfect example of this and are full
of sandwich eaters sitting on the grass. Walking about
the streets eating from a bag while shopping at the
same time has never really been acceptable.

Public transport is a grey area; some national bus
companies have banned it altogether, while some of the
more serious airlines openly encourage it by charging
for everything. Eating in public may not be the taboo it
once was and eating on the hoof is a necessity for some
people, so presumably if you bring a napkin with you and
don't leave your litter behind, change the general aroma
in the surrounding area or cause any offence to anyone
else, it now seems to be acceptable.

AFTER THE PARTY

CLEARING UP

This is the worst part; great night, great party, but, wow, the clearing up can be tedious. If you are up to it, do it all the same night, because getting up to face it the following morning is horrendous. However, you must do it after the party – not during – because doing serious cleaning while you should be looking after your guests is rude and defeats the purpose of inviting people in the first place.

Clear up with as much care and attention as the setting up in the first place. Collect everything up slowly and wash the glasses and cutlery first, then the plates if doing it by hand, or just stick the whole lot in the dishwasher: first load glasses and cutlery, then load the rest until it is all done. Dry up with bone-dry, immaculately clean, lint-free teacloths. A washing-up bowl full of warm water and washing-up liquid is very useful – tip the cutlery in to soak.

Never be in too much of a hurry to get the vacuum cleaner out. After a fantastic celebrity party a couple of years ago in the South of France I left the vacuuming to the cleaners for the following morning, which was just as well because as I left the building I stepped on a large, valuable diamond that had fallen out of an obviously precarious ring setting.

Some people swear by disposable plates when hosting a big party and then once used just bin them but, if you prefer to use real plates and glasses, designate a specific area where they can be stacked during the party and are ready for washing. Finding a spot will be a lot easier if you wash up and put away the pots and pans you used to prepare the food before your guests arrive. Load the dishwasher with heavy or cumbersome things so you don't have to hand wash them.

You can, if your budget allows it, rent china and glasses for the evening; sometimes you can arrange for the dirty china and glasses to be loaded back into the crates in which they arrived, and sent back to the hire company unwashed. Do check this service is available first though.

Don't stack dirty things in the sinks, it not only looks horrible but the sink is one of the most important resources in the kitchen and having to do things when it is full up with dirty plates is annoying. The sink should be empty and clean at all times.

If you have allowed smoking in your house during the party don't just throw the filthy contents of the ashtrays straight into the bin. Wrap the whole lot up in a length of aluminium foil and leave it in the sink until the following morning. That way you reduce the fire risk and the house won't stink of old fag ends either.

Clean up and check for any stains on table linen, carpets or furniture. The sooner you do this the better in some cases. Collect up and pack any useful leftovers and if needs be refrigerate them and discard the rest. Then clean the kitchen floor.

HANGOVERS

A hangover is the miserable nauseating feeling caused by the over-consumption of alcohol and made much worse by the over-consumption of tobacco at the same time. Medical science hasn't, as yet, come up with a useful solution except for drinking less alcohol. However, the following suggestions may be useful:

• Eating before you drink alcohol is always a help, as is a glass of milk. Both slow the absorption of alcohol into the bloodstream.

• It may be boring for some, or even impossible for others, but sticking to the same drink all evening has long been advised, since mixing some drinks can have disastrous side effects.

- Alcohol causes dehydration because it's a diuretic – and so is coffee – so the over-consumption of coffee during the evening adds to the general horrible feeling. The old idea that drinking black coffee acted as some sort of antidote is unfounded. Instead, drink plenty of water. Drink water before going to bed and have water close by to quench the thirst in the middle of the night. It is dehydration that causes that trembling feeling.

- An irritated stomach may produce acid, and to combat this some over-the-counter antacid medicines can be helpful. Mineral waters are alkaline as well as being thirst quenching, so they are doubly useful.

- Fructose helps the body to metabolise alcohol. It also replaces blood sugar, which will be low the morning after. Low blood sugar makes for that weak hollow feeling. Vitamin C helps the liver detoxify the blood and B vitamins are also thought to be beneficial.

Hair of the dog

It is believed by some people that drinking a small amount of alcohol the morning after the night before can have a beneficial effect on a hangover and is possibly the reason why a Bloody Mary was invented. However, the bad news is that the relief is only temporary. The liver attacks poisons in a certain order, with ethanol first. Once all the ethanol has been broken down it starts on the methanol, which releases formic acid into the system and makes the feeling worse. Hitting the liver with another dose of ethanol stops it processing methanol and it starts on the new threat – but the methanol will have to be processed at some time so the hangover is only being postponed until later.

Hair of the dog

The expression comes from the phrase 'a hair of the dog that bit you', in other words a little bit more of the alcohol that caused the hangover in the first place.

Long Island Iced Tea

There are clearly many who believe in the efficacy of the morning-after drink and the stronger and earlier the drink the better, as I am often asked for a gin and tonic at seven-thirty in the morning.

But my favourite so far was an American who, clearly suffering badly from too much Champagne the night before, asked me for a 'Long Island Iced Tea' instead of breakfast. Not being altogether sure whether we had that particular variety of tea in stock I politely suggested one that I knew we had. 'No, no', she said noticeably trembling. 'Just bring me a large glass with some gin and white rum, Tequila, Cointreau, vodka, some ice, a bottle of very cold cola and a slice of lemon.' So I did and then watched as she downed the whole thing in one go. I can't be sure if it had the desired effect but it certainly put the colour back in her cheeks.

HOW TO BE
A GOOD GUEST –
AND GET
INVITED BACK

Answering invitations

The abbreviation RSVP, of course, comes from the French '*Répondez s'il vous plait*' meaning 'Please respond'. If RSVP is written on an invitation it means the invited guest must tell the host whether or not they plan to attend the party. It does not mean respond only if you are not going to attend and it does not mean only respond if you are.

It means the host wants a definite head count for the planned event and needs it by the date on the invitation. An incomplete list of respondents can cause quite a few problems for a host, including difficulty in planning food and drink quantities, or difficulties in planning appropriate seating. It's also about being polite and it's good to know who is coming, so the next time you see RSVP on your invitation, do just that – respond.

Replies to fairly informal private events such as a dinner party at home or a garden party should be handwritten and addressed only to the hostess and sent within ten days or so of the event, but really the sooner the better. Traditionally written in the third person and without a salutation, an example would be as follows:

> *Mr David Jones thanks Mrs John Smith for her kind invitation to dinner on the 10th of May and looks forward to attending / regrets that he is unable to attend.*

This is the correct way to do it but it could be seen as a little too formal or stiff for the average party, so if there is an email address or a telephone number on the invitation, it is perfectly in order to reply using either. If the invitation invites you and a guest then your reply should specify the name of the guest you are bringing. If your invitation actually names the person with whom you will be attending and you have to change the name for any reason only do this after a check with your hostess that it is in order to do so; this is not only polite but could avoid any unexpected embarrassing meetings.

More formal invitations require a more formal response and in the case of a wedding invitation one should respond by writing in the third person without a salutation or a signature. Address the envelope to the bride's mother but refer to both of the bride's parents in the reply. The date you reply should be written at the bottom of the page:

> Mr David Jones thanks Mr and Mrs Smith for
> the invitation to the marriage of their daughter Jane,
> to Mr John Brown at The Church, Clifton,
> on Saturday 10th May at 2 o'clock and reception
> afterwards at The Grand Hotel and is pleased to
> accept / regrets that he is unable to attend.

When, and if, you have to decline an invitation to a less formal affair you should try to give as much notice as possible and if you want to you may offer a reason; you may be believed or you may not but correct form says you should decline as gracefully as possible.

Who else is going?

You shouldn't really ask who else is going, however tempting it may be; just try to be pleasantly surprised when you turn up. You could ask about the style or formality of the event; that way you can adjust your outfit and you might just elicit the names of others on the guest list without causing any offence.

Dressing up

On formal invitations there will be a note about the dress code somewhere and if there isn't try to ask around to find out what you will be expected to wear. If the invitation states Black Tie or even Black Tie Optional take it that they mean wear it. For men that's a tuxedo or dinner jacket and a black bow tie and for women, it means classic evening dress. I have seen a variety of evening dress worn at some very formal parties from cocktail dresses to ball gowns so it is best for women to check out what is *en vogue*.

Follow what the invitation asks for. Turning up for a bash in the Shires in the middle of winter in a white jacket at a black tie event as if for dinner with the captain on a cruise ship does look rather out of place and you could be mistaken for one of the band.

There are strict guidelines for those invited to formal events hosted by the Armed Forces; it will probably be clear on the invitation but if you are in any doubt at all, you really should ask to avoid any embarrassment.

Introducing yourself

Once at the party and in the door, drop off your gift if you have one (see page 154) and then, should the situation arise, introduce yourself as you shake hands with other guests. Leave out the honorific, so don't say for example 'Hi I'm Mr, Dr or Mrs'; just your first name is fine. If the other person is a casual acquaintance you should never assume they will remember you, so remind the other person where you last met.

A three-way introduction, where you introduce two other people to one another, is slightly different and to be polite you should proceed as follows. This is especially the case in a business setting where you should, to show due deference, start with the most senior-ranking person, for example:

> *Dr Smith, I'd like to introduce to you my colleague Mr John Brown who started with us yesterday. John this is Dr Jane Smith.'*

This sounds a little formal but in a formal environment it is perfectly correct. In this case it would be prudent for *John* to start calling *Dr Jane Smith* by her last name and not assume he can immediately call her *Jane* until invited to do otherwise.

In a business setting knowing how to do this properly can be very important and introductions should match, so if you only know the first name of one person you should say the first names of both. If you add an honorific for one person then you should add one for both.

What to bring?

Gifts

Taking a small gift for the host is a kind thing to do and although not expected it can seem a little thoughtless or mean not to. Certainly if you are staying overnight a gift of some sort should definitely be offered and if you are invited for Christmas lunch you really should not turn up empty-handed.

What you choose to take is clearly up to you and taking a bottle to a party, if it is acceptable, has long been a standard offering, but there is no reason why you can't be more inventive. Take something that you know the hosts like and will appreciate. Italians I have worked with bring locally produced olive oil or jars of compote made from local produce, which is a nice personal touch and always seems to go down well. At a very arty London gathering, one of the guests brought the host a lamb chop, which he produced from his pocket and although it wasn't wrapped it was very well received. For a much grander affair in Hampshire, a couple who had jetted in from Vienna just for the evening, arrived carrying a traditional Viennese *torte* in a very elaborate box festooned with bows and ribbons. Once opened, the cake was found to have become squashed flat during the journey but the gesture was much appreciated. Hand the gift to the host or hostess on arrival or if they are not there to greet you, leave your gift near the entrance.

Flowers

Smart and classy, flowers are guaranteed to fit every occasion and always make an impression.

Take a bunch of fresh flowers from your garden if you have one and there is something worth cutting; it's a very personal thing to do. A bunch of sweet peas or a vase of rhododendrons for the dining room makes a lovely gift.

If you don't have a garden or it's out of season take a reasonable-sized bunch from a good florist. Hand pick the selection if you know the person well and you know their favourites.

Lilac for some strange reason is thought to be unlucky by some people, if cut and brought into the house. My grandmother would never bring ivy into the house for the same reason.

As for colour, white flowers are linked with purity and therefore often reserved for funerals and sympathy. People from Thailand use antirrhinums for funerals and the Italians, the French and some other Europeans associate chrysanthemums with all things funereal. Rosemary is for remembrance of course. Yellow flowers are for good friends but keep red roses for your Valentine and give dark blooms to men – black tulips are a very good example.

Handbag etiquette

Ladies should never put a handbag on the dining table at any time during dinner and certainly never on the loo floor or any floor for that matter. Indeed, those who follow the workings of Feng Shui, a 3,000-year-old Chinese system of aesthetics, also believe it to be very unlucky to put a handbag on the floor. This has to do with respect for what could be in the handbag and is presumably a reference to money.

With some genuine designer handbags carrying phenomenally high price tags, top restaurants these days offer a handbag stool to keep the masterpieces off the floor during dinner.

Mobile phones and laptops

Unless you happen to be a medic on call or the prime minister, turn your mobile phone off at parties. If you have left it on, never answer it during a conversation and never put it on a dining table while you eat. Same goes for laptops; there's a time and a place and dinner isn't one of them.

Table manners

Sitting down at a table faced with stacks of cutlery and glasses is not everyone's idea of fun and for the uninitiated it's definitely confusing. Dining shouldn't be a stressful thing, just relax – things are not as formal as they used to be and you won't find yourself banished for using the wrong spoon. If you really are unsure follow someone else, perhaps the host.

Knowing how to behave at the table is still important; as people do watch others eat and can make judgements about you from the moment you lift your fork. In the case of a formal dinner party the basics still apply. Start from the outside and pick up the next piece of cutlery for each subsequent course, sit up straight, keep elbows off the table, eat and drink slowly, and bring your fork to your mouth rather than dropping your head.

Eating canapés

To avoid any embarrassing moments, eat canapés in one mouthful. Only pop one in if you are sure you are not about to be engaged in conversation or introduced to someone because you shouldn't really chew and talk. Avoid things that might be difficult to eat or cause any embarrassment, such as dropping bits on the floor or getting pieces of puff pastry stuck to your cheeks. Don't put a spoon that you have used back on the tray and never dip a half-eaten canapé into the communal sauce bowl. Although it might be very tempting never take more than one canapé at a time and overfill your mouth.

Departure

Oh, this is so basic it barely needs a mention, but like so many other things, thanking comes with its own rules.

Go and find the hosts when you are ready to leave and perform the same rituals as those performed on arrival, a kiss on each cheek or a handshake – that is, if you can still see straight! There is nothing worse than just clearing off without saying goodbye; it's a bit of a slap in the face rather than a kiss.

If there are two or more hosts, thank each one individually; to miss one out would be wrong. Don't keep them hanging around at the door with prolonged goodbyes; they have a party to attend to.

If you really enjoyed the bash, send a card to the host to say so and thank them again. If the event was connected with work there is no reason why you shouldn't follow it up by thanking the host with a quick email.

INDEX